GREAT
OPPORTUNITIES

Marty Friedman

Inc.
Bellingham, WA

GAMZU Inc.

Bellingham, WA

Library of Congress Control Number: Pending

ISBN: 979-8-9890213-3-8 (Paperback)
ISBN: 979-8-9890213-4-5 (Audiobook)

Design by Melissa Vail Coffman

Praise for Marty Friedman

"Marty's a legend in the industry. He reminds me of my grandfather, A.J. Richard, in the way his business became his love and his passion.

"Marty's Eastern Marketing people come into our stores and promote their products to our people on the sales floor. They educate and teach us the selling points and features of their products, and they help our people to feel comfortable about selling those products.

"They don't make them like Marty anymore, with the drive and the passion, and the love for the business. When it comes to Marty Friedman, this is one time when the nice guy finished first."

—Gregg Richard, P.C. Richard & Son,
President, owner, 65-store retailer

"There is no one that will ever work in my company that will not be required to read it. Marty's book is truly a 'North American' blueprint of the distribution business."

—Don Redman, Redman Distributing,
CEO, owner; Cambridge, Ontario, Canada. Distributor for Bertazzoni,
Vent-A-Hood, Alfresco, and formerly Marvel, and AGA

"Over my 40 years in the home appliance industry, I have leaned on our major distributors, dealers, and retailers for advice on new products and on new marketing strategies. Marty was often the only one on the other side of the equation. He and Craig have been critical to the success of our products and marketing programs. Read this book for the lessons it teaches about being successful in both business and life. Marty has led an amazing life and has left his indelible mark on the industry."

—Gordon Stauffer, former owner of Marvel Refrigeration;
former President of Fedders Corp, Chairman, AHAM
(American Home Appliance Manufacturers Association)

"Thank you, Marty, for sharing your many years of experience and wisdom. These stories are endearing and provide us with many lessons we can pass on to our children so that they become the next generation of successful entrepreneurs."

—MIKE EDWARDS, former CEO and President of **Lynx Professional Grills**, President, Commerce, CA. Luxury gas grills

"When you meet Marty, you get that immediate understanding that he knows the business. If, like me, you have been lucky enough to work with Marty, you can learn from him. If you never had that opportunity, read his book."

—PAOLO BERTAZZONI, **Bertazzoni,**
CEO and owner, Guastalla, Italy.
Cooking appliances made in Italy since 1882

"As a second generation of leadership at Redman Distributing Inc., I was intrigued to read Marty's book. My life is very busy and time to read books often gets shelved. My father, Don Redman, read it and our company's Operations Manager, Dave Matchett, has already purchased every employee their own copy. It's a mandatory read for my company."

—DON REDMAN, owner of **Redman Distributors**, Tukwila, WA and Cambridge, Ontario, Canada. Distributor for Vent-A-Hood, Capital, Alfresco, & Marvel brands

"Marty is a larger-than-life character who has built an incredibly successful business on the principles in his book. He's an old school sales pro who doesn't take short cuts. Everything he has written in his book is the truth and he continues to outpace everyone around him. I should know, I work for him. He sent me his book to read but half of what is written in the book I have had the pleasure of experiencing firsthand working with him. He is tenacious and sharp as a whistle. I have 30 years of successful selling under my belt and I am a pro. That is why he hired me. Yet, I continue to be amazed at him."

—ALAN M.

I dedicate this book to all those people who taught me and helped me get ahead. Nobody gets there by themselves, and there are many people who made the difference and helped.

Unfortunately, when they were teaching me, I didn't appreciate what they were doing for me, and never thanked them.

We learn from others.

INTRODUCTION

I WAS A BOY WHO STARTED WITH nothing and finished with more than I ever wished for. I want to inspire others to do the same and to learn from my experiences. I recommend the appliance industry in retail sales first and then wholesale sales, or in the interior design area, as a great place to make your career.

As a young man, I always questioned if I'd be able to make my mark in the world because I didn't have the smarts or grades that most of my classmates had. I wasn't a good athlete which is what counts in grammar and high school, and my parents didn't have a lot of money. I did understand though that if I didn't do it for myself, there was nobody else to do it for me.

Today, I consider myself the luckiest person in the world. I am 96 years old.

I have a wonderful, loving family even though 10 years ago I lost my very special and supportive wife. I have two great sons, two wonderful daughters-in-law, and five smart grandchildren.

After 70 years in the TV & appliance business, I am still active in our family business and still love it.

I believe this statement: "If you do what you do, and love what you do, you shouldn't call it work."

My doctors say that I am in good health although I am not as strong, agile, or sharp as before. My physicians in Florida and in New Jersey say that I look 20 years younger than I am. I'm 5'10" tall. I weigh 162 lbs. I drive at night. I exercise for one hour three days a week. I watch what I eat. I have a full head of hair.

I hate the fact that I sleep 9 hours at night and a 2- or 3-hour every afternoon, but my doctors say that at my age sleeping a lot is good because it recharges you.

I listen to inspiring audio books. Every month I read Forbes magazine and Fortune Magazine and Bottom Line Personal.

I meet with my computer consultant every week for two hours and I learn more each time so I know more than just "Control C and Control V.

I try to keep up and with knowledge about our business. I try to know as much as our 11 full-time outside District Sales Managers and our 22 full-time inside salespeople.

I attend the major appliance exhibits like the KBIS Show in Las Vegas and Orlando, and the NECO Show in Providence, RI. and Mohegan Sun.

From time to time, I visit customers with one of our 11 District Sales Managers. All fun and enjoyed showing that I can still be effective.

This past year, I saw customers in many states in the eastern U.S., where we sell Bertazzoni kitchen appliances (Italy), Blomberg Kitchen Appliances (Turkey), and our trademark brand Xo product line, which includes:

- XO gas grills (previously Lynx, ProFire brands)

- XO range hoods (previously sold Zephyr, Rangaire, Nutone. All three were bought by Broan, who fired us)

- XO undercounter forced air refrigerators (previously Marvel)

- XO undercounter forced air wine cellars (previously Marvel)

- XO microwave ovens, (previously Sanyo, Sharp)

- XO ice machines (previously Marvel)

- XO garbage disposals (previously Waste King)

- XO refrigerated drawers (previously Sharp)

We were lucky to learn the business by selling other brands.

Why this updated version?

My original book, published in 2013 under the title "YOU CAN TOO," was well received. Many industry leaders, retailers, and salespeople said they loved the book and learned from it.

After 12 years, it was time for an update on for both print and audio.

It is also an opportunity to explain the changes in the industry and, at age 96, explain Marty Friedman's opinion of what everyone can do to live longer and healthier.

At a Young Age, We All
Need Encouragement

I COULD NEVER HAVE ACHIEVED ALL THESE blessings without help and inspiration from so many people along the way.

First, thanks to my mother, who always inspired me and promised me that I would be very successful. I feared that I could never compete because I couldn't in grammar school and high school. I assumed that all the smarter kids would always do better than me.

My mother would say that you will win if you work harder, work more hours, learn, and use your street smarts.

I also give thanks to my late wife for accepting all those days and nights alone with our two sons, while I pursued my goals in business.

She always gave me good business advice. She was great with the buyers' wives when we would get together for a dinner or a show.

Women have a sixth sense that men don't have. She always got along well with their wives. I learned that the wives of the buyers could say things to their husbands that nobody else could say. The owners or buyers were not so powerful when they were in the presence of their wives. The wife could interrupt their husbands and say something like: "Stop being so difficult with these nice people. I like them. I want them to be our friends and to see them again."

Those dinners helped me form better relationships. I never thought that going to the best restaurants and seeing the best Broadway shows and events with customers was work. That was all fun.

When I drove from one dealer to another, instead of wasting time listening to music in my car, I enjoyed listening to motivational speakers on my car radio with cassette tapes from some of my favorite motivational speakers:

Earl Nightingale, Brian Tracy, Zig Ziglar, and Tony Robbins.

A. J. Richard, the founder at P.C. Richard & Son taught me that the most important word that we can use in business is "WE." It's not "I." Don't be a big shot and think you did it all yourself. I learned and I recommend that everyone learns that lesson in order to be successful in this business or in any business. "We" and not "I."

My Early Years
Learning To Compete

IN GRAMMAR AND HIGH SCHOOL, I was the shortest and probably the weakest for my age in school.

I didn't start to grow until I was 15 and received weekly growth hormone injections from my family doctor. When I entered high school, I was 5' tall.

Our grammar school was next to the high school. On my first day of high school, one boy saw me in the hallway and told me that I was in the wrong school. He told me that the grammar school is next door. I was insulted, but he was right because I looked too young to be in high school.

I was unable to compete in athletics with others my own age.

When the weather was nice, in gym class we played softball. The two best athletes would alternately choose two teams. I would always be the last one and still not chosen by either team.

The gym teacher would say to one of the two captains that they get this last man.

That captain would say something like: "That's Friedman. We don't want him. He's. SH_T." The gym teacher would insist and then I would be assigned to right field. That was painful to hear. Even now it hurts to recall.

It is very difficult to not to fit in. Short people will all tell you that if you ask them.

To compensate in sports, I would practice at the school field for hours and hours. I practiced even when it was getting dark, and I would still be working at trying to get better.

I would frequently be late for dinner because I used to challenge myself to not leave until I could shoot 10 baskets in a row from the foul line, without missing any, and the same with my left-handed and right-handed hook shots.

I didn't realize it at the time, but I was teaching myself that if you work more than the competition, you can get better.

Later in my business I competed the same way because I had learned that by working more and harder, you win. I enjoyed the results, so to me it wasn't work.

Another problem for me was that my reading skills were poor. I was a slow reader with poor retention of what I read. I therefore hated to read or study. I guess I had never learned to read properly.

In high school the better students were always trying to get all "A's" so they could have a chance to be accepted to a good college where they could continue to get top grades and then be accepted to a medical school or a dental school.

There were quotas to limit acceptance of Jewish students, so that made it even more difficult to be accepted.

My high school grades were mostly Cs and maybe one D, and I understood that I could never be accepted in medical or dental schools because of my average grades.

My father influenced me in ways that I didn't realize until later in life. He demanded that I never lie.

When I was seven years old, a school friend, Mikey Picaroni, recommended that we break into a factory on a Sunday morning to see what they were making. He broke a window and climbed in. I followed after he taunted me that I was "afraid."

It was a factory that made small nail scissors. We took some and left.

When my father came home, I told him, and he beat the hell out of me, and explained that we don't steal, and I had to stay away from Mikey.

A few years later I learned that Mikey was sent to what they called "Reform School."

My father taught me that you earn by working hard, and that honesty and hard-work work.

He always got up early and left in his car for work at 5 a.m. in order to "miss the traffic."

He would say that being in slow, heavy traffic is a total waste of time, so I should avoid it. Therefore, when I went to work as a salesman, I always left my house at 6:30 a.m., when traffic was lighter. I always thought that when you make an appointment with someone, it's like signing a contract and when you are early, it shows that you are honoring your contract and showing respect to the person that you made the appointment with.

That's why I always try to arrive 10 minutes before the agreed time for any appointment.

Dad's job in 1935-1945 was to buy fruits & vegetables at auctions from produce grown on farms in southern NJ. He would go to the farmers auctions that were held at places like the Vineland Cooperative Produce Auction in Vineland, NJ or a similar Co-op Auctions in Swedesboro, Glassboro, Hammonton, and Pitman on Monday to Thursday.

He would bid and buy farm grown baskets of produce, and he and his driver, would load the baskets and boxes on his truck "securely" and the driver would drive it to the Newark, NJ wholesale food market on Miller Street.

Then they would unload the fresh produce on the street and his salesman would sell it to the many grocery stores and vegetable stores who would arrive that night.

Sales would start at 12 midnight and finish at about 8 in the morning. Today, the Vineland Cooperative is still operating, and Wikipedia says that Vineland ships 80 to 90 trailers of fruits and vegetables every weekday and 200-300 trailers-loads on Saturdays and Sundays. I thought it was a great business. My father said that it was not for me because he wanted me to be a doctor where I would be respected.

When I was 13 years old, my father took me to the farmer's auction 96 miles away in Swedesboro, NJ.

That morning Dad stopped at a farm before going to the Swedesboro Auction.

This was in 1943 during World War II when there were shortages of many items like butter, sugar, and cigarettes. You could buy them only with a government certificate.

Dad asked the farmer if he smoked Lucky Strike cigarettes. The farmer said, "Yes."

Dad said: "That's good. Then maybe you could do me a favor. Everybody knows that I smoke only Camels. Some guy told me that he could get me Camel cigarettes, but he made a stupid mistake and he got me sixteen cartons of Lucky Strikes. Maybe you could you help me out and take them off my hands?"

Then Dad opened the trunk of his car to show a big cardboard container with 16 cartons of Lucky Strikes cigarettes. It filled most of the trunk.

The surprised farmer replied, "Are you sure Charlie? How much do you want for them? "Nothing," dad said. "They're of no use to me and you'd be doing me the favor taking them off my hands."

The farmer looked in the trunk and said "absolutely. I'll take them."

Then he carried the big carton into his kitchen and invited us in for a cup of coffee. After coffee, dad asked if he could see the farmer's fruits and vegetables that he already had on his truck and scheduled to go to the auction that morning. After some discussion, dad asked how much the farmer expected to get for everything that was on the truck for today's auction sale. After a little negotiation Dad bought the whole truckload.

I learned that people will take something if they think that it costs the other party little or nothing. Then they always respond by giving something back in return. That's good business. Sometimes it's good to give a little to get a little.

On another trip to Vineland, we drove in dad's brand-new maroon four-door Pontiac sedan, and again we stopped to see a farmer. New cars were still in short supply. Dad always bought a model that was still on the showroom floor because that meant that it was an unpopular model and Dad was sure that he could negotiate a better deal and get rid of his trade-in. That's the reason that our family car was always maroon or dark green, the least popular colors. He always eliminated wasting time buying the new car that way.

Looking at Dad's new maroon four-door Pontiac, the farmer said something about how he could see who was making all the money in this business because we drove up in this new car.

Dad's quick response was, "This car? You think I bought it? No. It's an unbelievable story but a farmer who I know, asked me to support his church and buy a $20 raffle ticket for his Catholic Church's fund raiser. It's must have been a miracle, but believe it or not, I won. I won this new maroon Pontiac."

Then the farmer laughed and said, "You are one lucky guy, Charlie. You aren't even Catholic!" The story wasn't true, but it seemed to satisfy everyone. Another lesson learned: don't leave room for jealousy or mistrust to creep in and poison a good relationship.

Boy Scouts of America

When I was 13, I joined the Boy Scouts of America, Troop 22. We would meet every week at my local grammar school after school. The 40 or 50 boys worked together. We learned honesty, integrity, patriotism, love of the outdoor life, and to do good for others. All great values that made me proud.

We learned emergency first aid, how to tie ropes, the names of knots, the Morse code used to send messages, and compass- and map-reading. We learned how to start a fire without matches and how to carry injured people. I loved everything about the Boy Scouts.

I respected my uniform, which I always kept neat and pressed. I loved it when we marched in the parade with bands downtown on Broad Street in Newark. I still remember the Boy Scout Law "A scout is Trustworthy, Loyal, Helpful, Friendly, Courteous, Kind, Obedient, Cheerful, Thrifty, Brave, Clean, and Reverent." Although most other guys my age left the Boy Scouts at the age of 15 or 16, I stayed to work towards higher achievement goals until I was 19. I learned to be in charge and be appreciated by my younger troopers.

Running is Great Exercise
For Your Heart

O NE SUMMER, WHEN I WAS 12 years old, my dad rented a house in the summer for the family in Bradley Beach, New Jersey. The house was 5 blocks away from the beach. It cost less to rent two rooms if it was further away from the ocean, and five blocks away was as far as it gets. We walked there and back every day. I was thrilled to be there.

However, the joy of being at the seashore didn't last long. While I was playing tag under water in the ocean I was kicked in the head. The next day, the Ears, Nose and Throat doctor said that I couldn't go into the water for the rest of summer.

That's when I decided that maybe this was telling me that it was time to start to build up my undersized body. So instead of walking to the beach, I taught myself to jog. Running in 1941 was not popular.

At first, I could run for only 20 feet and get out of breath. Then 50 feet. Then more distance and more distance.

I learned that there was suffering involved, but you tough it out and you win. I have been a jogger ever since.

Later in life when I was in the business world, whenever I traveled for factory visits, sales conventions, or a vacation, I would always be out jogging at dawn, which is when nobody else is on the streets.

It gave me the opportunity to run very early in the morning, when most people are still sleeping. You can see sights that you can't see when it's crowded. Ask anyone who jogs early in the morning before the world wakes up and they will tell you that it's a magical time.

I remember how exciting it was to jog in Japan from the hotel to find the Pacific Ocean which to my amazement looked just like the Atlantic Ocean.

In Sedona, Arizona, I was enchanted with those spectacular, memorable red mountains. I was always invigorated to run on North Michigan Avenue in Chicago from the beach area to the bridge and then back with no people on that busy main street.

Same thing on the coast of California in Laguna and Dana Point and at Newport, R.I.; Cape Cod; Milan; Italy; Korea; Taiwan, and many more places.

When I was 49, the doctors at the Delray Medical Center Emergency Room in Florida, said that it was a miracle that I survived 15 hours with a heart attack before they saw me. I had indigestion starting at 9 a.m. playing golf. Since I still had the indigestion at 3:30pm, I drove with my wife to the Emergency Room at the Delray Medical Center hospital.

The doctor tested me with a cardiogram and asked when I first had the heart attack. I told him that I wasn't there for a heart attack, I was there because I had indigestion. He said that my indigestion is a typical symptom of a heart attack and the cardiogram proved that I had a heart attack, but, "Nobody lives 15 hours with a heart attack," he said. But I did and that was amazing. He said that I survived only because my runner's heart was so strong.

When the surgeon arrived at 5:30 a.m., they gave me anesthesia and surgically inserted two stents in my heart valves to solve my problem. In my opinion, my decision to jog that summer was the foundation for my good health.

High School Graduates Don't Know
What Career They Should Choose

After I graduated from high school, I had no idea what I would like to do for my career. I applied to Drew University in Chatham, New Jersey and was shocked that they rejected me.

They said that my reading skills were not good enough for college. They recommended that I attend an 8-week speed reading course that was given that summer at Rutgers University in Newark. I attended Rutgers and after 8 weeks, I finally could read properly and my comprehension greatly improved. I was anxious to prove that I could compete academically now that I could finally read properly.

Then I applied and was accepted to Fairleigh Dickinson University in NJ.

My first day at school I was studying in my dormitory room when a group of my roommates and others came in and told me that it's not study time, it's "Party Time." Time for fun; for drinking beer and having a good time.

Apparently, we were not there for the same reason. I had something to prove and they were there to have fun. The next day I moved out or the dorm into a private residence where I could study. I could not afford to allow "Party Time" to interfere with proving that I could be at the head of all my classes.

At Fairleigh Dickinson, I did become one of the best students in every class I attended. I was very proud of myself.

My English & Public Speaking teacher was great and very helpful. She was from Ohio and initially recommended that I correct my New Jersey accent which she said would help me. I didn't realize that I had an accent, or that there was such a thing as a New Jersey accent, but she was right.

I learned and changed.

She taught me to say "OR-inge" instead of "ARE-inge,"

"FLOOR-id-duh" instead of "FLAR-uh-duh,

"FOR [4] instead of FAW like PAW,

"WHAT er" instead of "WAU tah,"

"BAHSTON" instead of "BAUWston."

She helped me with my diction, grammar, and recommended that I expanded my vocabulary and learned every day to use new words from the Thesaurus.

I made a terrible mistake because I never thanked her for helping me.

Good teachers are definitely under-appreciated.

I especially loved my classes in English, Voice & Diction, and Public Speaking. We were required to practice speeches in front of the class. When they gave me the microphone, I was so nervous that I was shaking. My speech was on something that I was very familiar with and I had written notes to help me.

It was recorded on a reel-to-reel tape recorder so that we could hear it later to learn and to improve. With repetition and training, it got easier and I got better. Practice does make perfect.

That year, I accomplished being an outstanding student. I was proud of myself for proving that I could compete academically. Life was good.

1948: As a Student at Fairleigh Dickinson University.

The Military Helps
Young People To Grow Up

While I was at Fairleigh Dickinson, my friends and I enlisted in the Army National Guard, 50th Armored Division. We avoided being drafted and going overseas to fight in the war in Korea.

That summer we traveled by train 100 miles north to an inactive army facility, Fort Drum, in Watertown, New York. We scrubbed floors, cleaned toilets, washed windows, cleaned sinks, and marched and marched

Then we experienced Boot Camp training which included watching the tanks with their target practice shooting shells that made our ground shake.

The bayonet practice with hand-to-hand training, was scary too.

Our non-commissioned officers were former soldiers from World War II. They loved having "the opportunity" to teach these young college students about military life and the Army rules. In civilian life our sergeants and corporals were people who worked as clerks at food markets or they worked at low-income jobs. They were thrilled to have the opportunity to teach us.

It was a painful experience for me, but I learned a lot. It changed my attitude about looking for the easy way. Military life taught me there are no shortcuts, only detours. Overall, this was a very beneficial experience that helped me to do better in life. I remained in the National Guard for eight years, including transfers to the Massachusetts Air National Guard at Logan Airport in Boston, when I was attending New England College of Optometry, and at Floyd Bennett Field in Brooklyn, when I transferred to the New York Air National Guard when I was back in New Jersey.

I received my honorable discharge in 1956.

I would recommend a year or two of military service for every young person because it teaches so much and helps young people to grow up.

Few Know What Job or Profession to Choose When They Graduate High School

MOST OF OUR BEST HIGH SCHOOL men students worked hard to get the best grades so they eventually could be accepted to a medical school or a dental school. My bad grades eliminated any opportunities like that for me.

Someone recommended Optometry. My father thought that was a perfect idea to be a doctor and a professional. I could become an eye doctor examining eyes, discovering diseases, examining for the best prescription for the best vision, and fitting for contact lenses. I applied and was accepted at the New England College of Optometry in Boston.

One of my three roommates in Boston was from Rumford, Maine. He was Catholic, and of French-Canadian heritage. He told me that in his home town of Rumford, they called him and his people, the derogatory name of "Frogs."

I never realized that and was so surprised to learn that there was prejudice against French Canadians. I always thought that prejudice was only against Jewish people, the Irish, and the Blacks. But I guess no group is immune. People can be mean.

When I arrived in Boston, I was finally 5'10" tall and I was accepted as a freshman to play for the New England College of Optometry basketball team. I played for the team for 4 years and in my last two years, I was the second highest scorer. That's not bad for the ex-short guy who was never chosen to play as a boy.

I was a good player because of all those extra hours practicing at the high school field by myself. When we played the New England College of Pharmacy, I was the leading scorer with 19 points.

On Monday, June 17, 1951, we played in the Boston Garden as the preliminary game against Cury College from Milton, MA.

In the featured game, the Baltimore Bullets won over the Boston Celtics by a score of 85 to 76.

Massachusetts College of Optometry basketball team.

The Celtics players included guard 6'1" Bob Cousy, the center was 6'8" Easy Ed Macauley. Also playing center was 6'10" Harry Boykoff. Guard Sonny Hertzberg was 5'10" tall, and 6'5" Chuck Cooper was the first African American player to be signed in the NBA, (from the Harlem Globetrotters). The second African American player drafted from the Harlem Globetrotters was 6'8" Nate "Sweetwater" Clifton, who signed with the New York Knicks.

We dressed for the game in the Boston Garden's locker room. It was exciting.

I scored three points against a really good team who had apparently selected us because they wanted to make sure that they would look good. They did.

Mass. College of Optometry	G	F	TP	N. E. College of Pharmacy	G	F	TP
Tacelli, rf	0	5	5	Faulkner, rf	4	0	8
Eiduks, lf	12	2	26	Shapiro, rf	2	1	5
Friedman, c	7	5	19	Cort, lf	0	0	0
Borsky, rg	4	0	8	Kaplan, c	4	0	8
Kaplan, rg	2	0	4	Puval, rg	4	2	10
LaChance, lg	6	1	13	Feldman, rg	7	5	19
Green, lg	0	0	0	Motyka, lg	1	0	2
				Tassinari, lg	10	0	20
	31	13	75				
					32	8	72

1951 Box Score Basketball Team

We played a game against the Harvard Medical School, at their gym on Huntington Avenue. When we arrived at their gym the lights were out. Our manager went inside and found that they had forgotten that they were scheduled to play us that night, but he said that he would "round up the guys" and be ready shortly.

On the first play, their 6'3" center outjumped our 6'6" center. He batted the ball to his teammate who raced past everyone and scored easily. They were great. At halftime, I said to one of the Harvard Med. students who was watching: "Your team is great, especially that number 14."

"Correct," he said. "That #14 was also great when he was a nationally ranked player at the University of North Carolina."

In those days, many of the best college athletes didn't go to the professional ranks, because it didn't pay that much, and financially they could do much better as physicians or dentists if they had good grades.

That taught me that appearances can be deceiving and to never to be overconfident.

Our Dean Ralph Green's lectures were practical and valuable.

He taught us to always use medical terms with patients to show that we were trained professionals.

ETIOLOGY is the cause of a disease.

PROGNOSIS is the expectation of the problem.

IDEOPATHIC is the term that means "without a known cause."

He taught us to always be in control of the situation by displaying confidence and knowledge. He taught us to act as professional as possible so we would be respected as professionals.

Professor Otto Hockstadt, an M.D., was from Germany. He was our Anatomy teacher. He required us to memorize the 12 cranial nerves and then the muscles of the body, because that was often asked on the tests for the State Licensing Boards of Examinations for medical and for optometry degrees for most States. He recommended that we do "Mnemonic learning." That is a memory device that aids information retention. I still remember it.

For the 12 Cranial nerves, we learned: "On Old Olympus Towering Tops, a Fin and German Vend Some Hops."

O-**Ol**factory, O-**Op**tic nerve, **O**-Oculomotor, **T**-Trochlear, **T**-Trigeminal, etc.

That's called "mnemonic learning—a devise that assists in memorizing something." The first letter indicates the first word that needs to be retained for the familiar memorable sentence.

For example, a famous mnemonic for learning the guitar strings names for guitar tuning is [from bottom string to top string]: **E**very **A**verage **D**ude **G**ets **B**etter **E**ventually.

We interned at the eye clinics at Massachusetts General Hospital, at Brigham & Women's Hospital in Boston, and at the New England College of Optometry Eye Clinic on Beacon Street.

Despite all my training and skill, on graduation day, my

roommate asked me: "Do you really like this stuff?" I said, "I'm not thrilled with it, but I guess being a doctor is a good thing and you can always make a living."

It was amazing to me that after four years, we still weren't sure about our chosen careers. You never know if you will like it, until you try it. We graduated in June 1952.

After I easily passed the New Jersey Optometry Association test, I began my practice as Doctor Friedman. My office was on Clinton Ave and High Street, Newark, NJ, across the street from the Riviera Hotel.

1954 Dr. Friedman's office in Newark, NJ.

Over the next two-and-a-half years, my patients said that I was the best. They said that I did the most thorough examinations and got the best results. A walk-in patient told me that he was there just to get a pair of reading glasses. I'm proud to say that, using my ophthalmoscope, I discovered that the patient had an advanced case of glaucoma.

I found the days to be boring. I didn't enjoy being in my small office all day long, seeing only a few patients. The patients were not interesting. The money was not that rewarding.

Too many patients believed that the ophthalmologists who did surgery were better qualified to do "refractions" to determine the correct eye glass prescriptions. To them, I was a second-class citizen and nothing I could do or say could change their opinion.

I decided that this professional field was not for me and not something that I would enjoy doing for the rest of my life.

People that I trusted told me that wholesale sales with a manufacturer or distributor in any field, is a good way to go. Wholesale not retail.

So, with my medical background, I applied for a sales position with a major pharmaceutical company in Manhattan. The interviewer told me that everything looked good on my application, until he got to the part about college.

"What's this about being a doctor? "I said "I am a doctor, but I don't like it and people tell me that I would be good in wholesale sales.

Then he said that he couldn't hire me because my application said I was a doctor. They were concerned that I would not stay with them long term.

He recommended that I apply to any other pharmaceutical company and not mention Optometry on the application. Then I would definitely be hired.

He recommended that I say that I attended Northeastern University in Boston, and graduated after 4 years with a BS degree. If you tell them you graduated from the New England College of Optometry, no pharmaceutical company will hire you because they think you will return later to your original profession.

I applied to another pharmaceutical company in Manhattan anyway.

When I filled out the application, and got to the part about education, I paused and decided that I would not lie to get a job. They told me the same thing about not accepting me. That's when I decided to find a wholesale selling job in something not so medical. Maybe they don't deserve me.

I asked my mother what she would think if I left optometry for a career in wholesale sales. She said that I should follow my dreams and to do whatever I thought was right for me.

My father said that I couldn't leave at that time. "You just got started. You have an office, the best equipment, a great location, and everyone says that you do a great job examining their eyes and getting them the perfect prescription," he said. "Nobody likes what they do. That's why they call it work."

I was now thinking about making a change and leaving optometry to find something that I would like to do.

Meeting The Girl Of Your Dreams, It Makes The Difference

ONE MONTH BEFORE I STARTED WITH the appliance distributor, I met a special girl named Corrine Blitzman. She lived with her parents one block away. Her aunt was one of my mother's best friends. I didn't know her before because in school I was short and she was tall.

We went on a blind date to the Chanticleer restaurant in Short Hills, the luxury restaurant in the area.

There was slow music and dancing and it was so romantic . . .. She was different from all the other girls I had ever dated . . .. I fell in love that night.

She was still available at age 25 only because her father said that she couldn't go to college because that was a waste of money. She enrolled in high school with the secretarial curriculum although all her friends were in the college curriculum. She learned shorthand, typing, stenography, and bookkeeping so she could be a good secretary.

In high school, she modeled part time at Bamberger's Department Store and worked after school for Golden Electric, the leading small appliance distributor, as the telephone operator and salesperson answering questions about models, inventory, delivery, and pricing.

After she graduated from high school she learned that she could not get the fifty-cents-an-hour raise that she requested, so she took a job in a one-person office for a roofing company that paid two dollars more an hour.

Corrine was alone there all day. Her best friends attended Syracuse University and all got married after graduation.

Corrine's goals and values were everything that I liked. She didn't have a rich father who would give her everything she wanted. Her mother worked. When I asked her about the possibility of my giving up on being a doctor to find something that I really liked, she said that I should do whatever makes me happy. "Money isn't everything," she said. She said that when we married, she would work and, "We can live on less if we have to until you do better."

That next month in the *Newark Evening News*, the announcement read that Corrine Blitzman was engaged to Dr. Martin Friedman, but a year later that same newspaper said that she married Mr. Martin Friedman.

A WHOLESALE SALES CAREER MAY NOT BE AS PRESTIGIOUS, BUT IF YOU ARE SUCCESSFUL AT IT AND LOVE IT, IT CAN BE VERY PROFITABLE

IN 1955, I INTERVIEWED WITH COOPER Distributing Co., a TV/appliance wholesale distributor in Newark. Cooper was not one of the most successful distributors because they were not selling the popular brands of TVs or appliances.

After reading my resume, the general manager said that in his opinion, I was too educated and too refined to succeed in this business. "Nobody in this business goes to college. Most of our people don't graduate from high school." He said that it is true that the top salespeople make a lot of money, but there are not many who can sell products that are hard to sell.

I said I would appreciate an opportunity to prove that I could be successful.

He said that my interview was only as a favor to a friend, but he was sure, after meeting me, that I would not succeed. Then he asked: "Are you really a doctor?"

"Yes," I said.

"What the ****, do you want with this business?"

He said that he would honor his promise to his friend and would hire me, IF I WOULD ACCEPT HIS TERMS:

For the first 30 days, I would work in the parts department, clean the floors, clean the appliances in the showroom, help in the parts department, answer telephones, help in the order department, and study their products and prices when I had time. For the first 30 days, I would receive **no pay.**

1955 Motorola Big Screen 19-inch color TV, only $999.

For the next 30 days, they would pay me $50 a week, which covered gas for the car.

I would be assigned a territory to sell Motorola TVs to retailers from the western border of Newark to the Pennsylvania border. Then later if I was successful selling Motorola, I could sell their Gibson refrigerators, International Harvester freezers, ABC washers and gas dryers, and Ampro tape recorders.

After the one-month trial period, if I didn't do good business, I would be fired. If a miracle happened and I did good business, I would be hired as a regular District Sales Manager on a salary and commission basis like their other five salesmen. My exclusive territory would be Essex, Morris, Warren, Sussex counties.

I said "Thank you for the opportunity."

My First Day on the
New Job in Wholesale Sales

THE FIRST RETAILER THAT I VISITED was about 10 miles west of the distributor's showroom on 177 Central Ave in East Orange.

The store owner's response to my presentation was: "Do you know that your Motorola TV prices are higher than RCA, GE, Zenith, Admiral, Dumont, Philco, Emerson, and Olympic? There is no demand for your product. Nobody asks for your brand. Your styling is old. Your products don't work as well as the other brands. Did you know that your company sold some Motorola models to the new discounter in town, Two Guys from Harrison, and that they are reported to be selling them at just above cost. You look like a nice clean-cut kid. Do yourself a favor. Find a real job. Nobody could sell this merchandise"

My second sales call was 5 miles west in Orange. This owner had the same negative report and recommendation.

I decided to seek my fortune in the furthest area of my new territory with the hope that possibly other territory salespeople may not go there that often.

I traveled 90 miles west on rural State Road 23 until I saw a store on the highway. It was Herbie's Furniture, with signs in the front window showing the top brands of furniture, mattresses, appliances and TVs. The store was big, active with consumers, and had all the popular brands

The owner listened to my sales presentation and repeated the same story that I had heard about my products from the previous two dealers. At least he didn't mention anything about Two Guys from Harrison. That was probably because they were very far away from Hamburg, NJ.

I decided to try and change the direction of the conversation and connect with him on a personal level. I told him that this was my first day on the job, the first time visiting this area, and that I didn't know this area at all.

"It's almost lunchtime and I hate to eat alone," I said. "I don't even know where any restaurants are located. I understand that you are not going to buy my Motorola brand, but I would like you to do me a favor and let me buy you lunch today? He thought for a minute, looked at the consumers in his store, and then responded, loud enough for everyone in the store to hear:

"NOBODY BUYS HERBIE LUNCH. Today, Herbie is buying YOU lunch."

Then we walked to his car and he drove us to a diner about 10 miles away on State Road 23. When we walked in, everyone gave Herbie a big hello.

I said, "It looks like everyone loves you. How do you get along with the people in the area, and in the diner?"

His response was: "They hate my guts."

Over lunch, Herbie told me his story. He had been an outside house-to-house route salesman for Barney's Furniture in Paterson. They gave him the worst territory—the far away western NJ area. That was in the days when house-to-house salesman would return weekly to the consumer's house to collect the $20 or $30 a week until the item was paid for, and then sell them another product from their catalog, again on terms.

After he had built up business with customers, and saved enough to open his own business, he did just that. He understood that there were no other home appliance & furniture retail stores within many miles of this location, and that he had an opportunity to create a successful business in far west, rural New Jersey.

During lunch he explained how he lived with his family 50 miles away in Paterson, NJ and left his house very early every morning to be at work when the store opened and he returned home every night from his store late.

His wife refused to move and raise their children in rural western NJ, where the business was located. He said everyone here hates my guts because I don't live in this area, because I don't belong to any of their Clubs, and I don't belong to their church. He said that he eats alone at the diner every day, and even though he gives the waitresses their biggest tips, they smile at him, but hate his guts.

I told him that I appreciated his courage for his efforts to work in such a hostile environment. Then I told him my story.

Herbie said that he was taking this abuse only because he was doing it to make a better life and future for himself, his wife, and his children.

We apparently had a lot in common.

When we got back to his car, after lunch, I asked him: "Herbie, since this is my first day in the business and since you know the business and I don't know the business, in your opinion, is there any way that these Motorola TVs could be sold?

He hesitated and thought for a moment.

Then he said, "Of course your product could be sold! Because it's not what you buy it for, it's what you can sell it for that really counts."

He went on to explain. Two days ago, he made a large sale to a new resident who just moved into town. The customer bought furniture, appliances, mattresses, and a TV.

The day after delivery, that consumer called him to tell him that he was a crook because that same model RCA TV that he bought from Herbie for $999. was being advertised in the New York Daily News for $650. He understood that he could have bought that same TV for $350 less. He said that Herbie probably overcharged him for everything. The customer said he will tell everyone that Herbie is a crook.

Herbie immediately called his factory representative and he was told:

"Herbie. Grow up. This is the business. That dealer in NYC is big. He buys everything cheaper because he's a much bigger user and he can sell our TVs for whatever he wants to sell them for. There is nothing that we can do for you. That's the business. If you don't like how we do business, you don't have to sell our products."

"Wow. What a story. So, what about my Motorola TVs. What do we do now?"

He said "I guess we go back to my office, and I give you your first order."

"IT'S NOT WHAT YOU BUY IT FOR, IT'S WHAT YOU CAN SELL IT FOR.

"Your Motorola TVs may not be well-known, or the best styled brand, but I can sell your brand for a profit because customers will buy it based on my recommendation. I know that it's not going to be advertised in the newspapers to embarrass me and make me look bad."

He then placed his first order for my Motorola TVs.

Herbie Sanders taught me how to sell merchandise that is not popular and, luckily, that was on my first day.

Anybody can take orders for the popular brands, but can the retailer make a fair profit selling those products?

HE TAUGHT ME HOW TO SELL WHAT THE CUSTOMER DOESN'T ASK FOR. Anyone can take orders for what the consumer is asking for.

Herbie smiled, "Kid, just listen to me. See your customers every week or so, NOT ONCE OR TWICE A YEAR, protect their profit with your merchandise, support your dealer, and you'll do just fine."

Thank you, Herbie, I will always be in your debt, and I'll always take care of my customers.

THE 2ND DAY OUT IN THE TERRITORY TRYING TO CREATE A BUSINESS

NEWTON, NEW JERSEY WAS ABOUT 80 miles away from my home base. There were no Interstate highways in 1955, just bad roads. On Main Street I saw Burt, the owner of the only store that had Motorola TVs on display. It was Sussex County Electronics on 30 Water Street.

Burt told me that he purchased those six Motorola TVs that are still on display as part of a promotion in order to qualify for a long weekend trip to Las Vegas, courtesy of the distributor. He and his wife had a wonderful time. He said that the owner of the distributing company is a wonderful generous guy. Everything was first class.

"But your Motorola products don't sell," said Burt. "They are more expensive than all the other brands. Their styling is old. They have no demand and no national advertising. They don't work well out here because of bad reception. Please tell Mr. Cooper that he has to take them back because I can't sell them and I certainly am not going to pay for them.

"You seem like a nice young man, why don't you get into another line of work."

I asked him if there was anyone in this town that he could recommend for me to see. He paused, smiling, he said: "There is always Joe Decker. Then he paused, but no, forget that idea. There is really nobody around here that makes sense for you."

I was desperate, "PLEASE. Please just tell me where I can find Joe Decker." Reluctantly, he directed me to a small TV repair shop with empty boxes of picture tubes stacked up outside the front window of the store.

I introduced myself as the new Motorola salesman for the area. He greeted me with, "Where have you been? How about showing me what you have?"

I opened my briefcase, took out my spec book, and showed him my products and their prices.

"Do you want to take an order?"

Excited, I took out my order pad, and Joe gave me an order for 12 Motorola TVs. He ordered two each of the first six models that I showed him. As I was filling out his credit application, I noticed that none of his suppliers was a TV manufacturer and there were no TVs on display in his store. I assumed that there must be a credit problem.

Burt then told me that I would probably need to know his story in order to get the merchandise shipped.

From the time he was in high school, he had always been good at fixing radios and TVs and installing TV antennas on top of the roofs.

While in high school, he got an after-school job doing what he did best—fixing TVs and installing antennas on rooftops for Gray's Department stores, which had three impressive stores. They were the largest seller of furniture and appliances in the area and they sold every top brand of furniture, bedding, TVs, and appliances.

After high school, Joe Decker joined the army to serve his country in the war in Korea.

Four years later he was discharged. With his discharge money, he decided that instead of going back to the three-store retailer, he would open his own TV repair shop and hopefully sell TVs. The big store prevented him from getting any TV merchandise to sell because they wanted him to return to work for them as their Service Manager.

So, he opened his little store anyway and repaired electronics and sold and installed rooftop antennas. The local residents loved Joe because they knew that he was the best in the area doing service and he was a good local guy.

He recommended that our credit manager speak with the credit manager at his parts distributor in Newark. They supplied him with the best Channel Master high power TV antennas which were needed for rural areas and RCA replacement picture tubes and parts, all from Aarron Lippman & Co, the parts distributor in Newark. They could verify that he does a good volume of business and always pays his bills promptly.

I took the order for the 12 Motorola TVs and after my last call of the day I drove to my distributor's headquarters in Newark to deliver the order to Murray, the Credit Manager, and told him Joe's story.

The sales manager complimented me on getting those two nice orders but cautioned me that we were still not sure the orders would be credit-approved and shipped.

One week later, when I went to those two accounts, I was hoping to see a few empty TV boxes outside each store which shows that some of the TVs were sold, but that wasn't the case.

When I came inside, I learned that Herbie and Joe both sold all of those TVs.

Both dealers gave me checks for payment and ordered even more TVs.

They recommended other dealers for me to see and sell.

They said their customers loved the Motorola TVs and that they were surprised that the products were so good and were priced so competitively.

The reason that Joe did so well was that the other local dealers priced their popular models TVs with a 35% profit plus the antenna, and Joe priced his Motorola TVs with the best Channel Master antenna with a 20% profit.

The local folks loved giving Joe a chance, and they trusted Herbie's recommendations.

I learned an important sales lesson; the right customer exists for every product. It is matching them up that makes all the difference in the world.

Enjoy Your Work

ICONTINUED MY SWING THROUGH WESTERN NEW Jersey seeing more retailers and telling my story. It was fun. I loved it. I had a better understanding of why retailers buy and understood that the popular brands paid attention mostly to the big retailers, and not the smaller ones. My business got better and better. I sold to Washington Appliance in Washington, NJ; Freund's Appliance, Succasunna, NJ; Alpha Radio in Alpha, NJ.

1958: Wife and son at first house.

The products improved in styling and performance and pricing.

I changed my vehicle from my gas-guzzling Oldsmobile 88 to a new blue Volkswagen Beetle that gave me 35 miles to the gallon instead of 13 miles to the gallon. I loved that little car.

Be Creative and Try New Things

MOST OF MY DAY WAS SPENT on long trips on narrow state roads in rural Jersey.

I noticed that many of the large billboards were empty or were used for public advertising like Fight Cancer, or United Way or Help the Boy Scouts. That meant free billboards for charities and empty ones too.

I called and met with the owner of that billboard company to explain what we did and that my Motorola manufacturer commits to money to advertising. But I proposed that we do a Test Program to prove that this advertising would work for TV manufacturers. I suggested that he give us six of his no profit billboards for three months AS A TEST and charge just for their printing and installing for $300 each to prove they would get good results. He agreed.

I got the dealers to pay $200 for each billboard with their name and address, on it. I got the distributor to pay the balance of $100 for each of the six billboards.

The billboards showed a picture of a Motorola TV, the Motorola logo, a catch phrase about the product, and the dealer's name and address on the bottom.

I selected the six best locations. It's amazing how consumers and the dealers were influenced by seeing the same billboards every day to and from work. Consumers told the dealers that they saw the Motorola ads on the billboards, and also on television, although the company never had TV advertising.

We gained credibility and recognition. The dealers also loved seeing their names on the billboards, and of course, the recognition of their stores.

That promotion helped us to become more of a major factor in rural western territory.

My company then asked me to travel to the Trenton territory to help build up that area. I was successful there, too, in increasing business. Next, they added the seashore territory. I was successful there in increasing business.

Then they asked me to help in the higher population, high-volume Passaic County area.

I found building the business with retailers and manufacturers, and the distributor, was easy and it was fun. It was like being the traveling preacher, helping the dealers to make more money and survive against the giant retailers. Being appreciated as the person who could make it happen was exciting and rewarding.

My first week I made my presentation to a dealer in Denville, NJ. After I finished, I was approached by a very successful distributor salesman who was listening to my presentation to the buyer.

He heard me talking about profitability and features and benefits, and how the retailer could make more profit selling our brands.

He told me that based on his experience as a successful salesman in the field, he wanted to do me a big favor and give me some valuable advice.

"You're going about it the wrong way." He said. "You need to lighten up. Dealers don't want to hear anything serious from their wholesale salesman." He advised me to tell them a couple of good jokes, talk about the Yankees and the Dodgers, and then tell the buyer about the weekly specials. "I can promise you that if you don't change, you'll never make it in this business." I thanked him for his advice. 20 years later he was working for me as a salesperson for my own sales agency company Marketing East.

1960: Flying to Zenith Distributor Convention in Chicago.

You Can Learn from People, Even if They Are Different

I WAS GIVEN THE HIGH-VOLUME PASSAIC COUNTY territory, including Lou Sales Appliance in Passaic, Goldberg's Appliance in Paterson, and Hammonds Appliance in Lodi.

Lou was a short, balding, brilliant man in his 50s. He was an entrepreneur selling appliances and televisions.

His knowledge of history, finance, and world affairs was spectacular. Every morning before work, he would read the entire *Wall Street Journal* and *New York Times*. He must have been college-educated, but he would never discuss anything about his personal life. He wouldn't tell me how he got into the business. It was quite an experience going to his store because he was always testing people to see how knowledgeable they were and how much mental abuse they would take in order to save money on a purchase, or just to do business with him.

He took delight in playing with peoples' minds, probing the extent of what they knew, and he enjoyed testing them.

Whenever I walked into his store and he was at the far end of the store, he would say to me in a loud voice something like:

"Welcome Dr. Pryzbyzywicz [PRIZ BIZ O WITZ]. I will be

with you in just a few minutes. How is your new washer and dryer working out?" Then he would say to everyone in the store: "You know that doctor is one the biggest heart specialists in the country." He understood the ethnic makeup of his market and thought that it made his customers happy to hear that an important doctor of Polish heritage was a customer of the Lou Sales' Appliance Store. Now that I think of it, it wouldn't surprise me to learn that he found the Dr. Prizbizowitz name in the *New York Times* or the *Wall Street Journal* and that there really was a Dr. Prizbizowitz . . . but not in NJ.

A day in Lou's store commonly went like this: he would ask a customer, "What are you looking for?" The customer might say: "a washer and a gas dryer." Louie would say: "How about this refrigerator?" Then he would point to a specific refrigerator. "I have a tremendous deal on these Whirlpool refrigerators today." When the customer would say, "No, just the washer and dryer," Louie would reply, "You see this 15-cubic-feet Whirlpool refrigerator? What if I told you that it was $199 today?" The average sale price for that model was probably $499.

When that customer would insist on just the washer and dryer, he would proceed to sell them just that. But everyone in the store would have overheard what he said about the sale and he hoped they would tell all their friends about HIS amazing low price. If someone later would ask to buy one of those $199 refrigerators, Louie would say, "I would like to buy them myself for $199. They cost me $350." He just wanted to see if that customer recognized a good value or not.

In the middle of the day, sometimes he would put a sign on the front door glass window that said: "Be back in 5 minutes for the Guaranteed Big Sale."

Customers would wait at the front of the store for him to return.

He might be gone for an hour to the bank to deposit cash, but people would still there be waiting for him and the Guaranteed Big Sale.

It was all part of his study to find out how long people would be willing to wait to save money. It was a fascinating learning experience for me. Most of the competitive wholesale salespeople would not tolerate his antics and wrote him off as crazy, and not being worth the effort. They would just call him on the phone and announce their specials, and take orders. But I was willing to take the nonsense and abuse and get much better results.

1965: Marty Friedman, age 36, Bachrach Studios, NYC.

I always got an order from Louie. I learned to go there at 5:00 or 6:00 p.m., first to get a check for his past due balance. That would never happen until after the doors closed. If there were still customers in the store, that meant staying later. Then he would write the check for what he owed, give me an order, and we would be off for dinner. He apparently had no friends and no relatives, and he hated to eat alone. Louie became my biggest customer.

When we were there alone, the telephone would ring and it was a consumer asking if the sale was still on. Lou would disguise his voice with a European accent and explain to the customer that he was the cleanup service person, but "what is it that you are interested in buying?" Then he would tell the consumer that he missed the BIG SALE AT LOU SALES APPLIANCE that was going on today. The crowds were so big that they had to call the police. "But if you are looking for a good deal on a refrigerator, they had the Whirlpool model XYZ on sale and if you give me the order now, I think I could get it for you." Something like that. He just loved to play with people's heads.

Because of his sales volume, in 1958, Louie was the only dealer invited and I was the only salesperson to be invited to the Motorola Distributor Convention at the brand-new Americana Hotel in Bal Harbor, Florida.

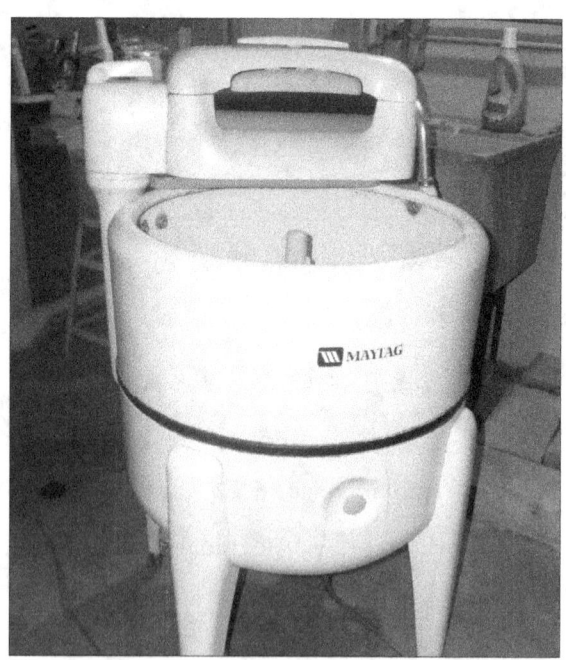

1956: Wringer washing machine.

He was my roommate. When he unpacked, I saw that he removed four identical blue blazer sports jackets from his suitcase. I asked him why he had four duplicates. His answer was simple. He liked that brand, that color, and that fabric.

At the hotel, we were waiting for an elevator when a beautiful tall young lady in her 30s waited with us. She towered over Louie. When the elevator arrived, she squeezed into the already crowded elevator. Louie reached up and touched one side of her face, moved very close and said: "Have you had anyone look at this recently?" She didn't move and didn't know what to do or say. Shocked, she said: "What do you mean?"

Then he appeared to examine her face with his face close to hers, then backed away, and said, "Please. Don't be alarmed. I'm a doctor. Let me see the other side." He then repeated his examination of her face, looking closely and touching both sides. "If I were you, I would definitely see your dermatologist about this as soon as possible." She said, "Thank you, doctor," and when the elevator door opened, she walked away.

Now you know why I used to refer to him as "Screwy Louie." You don't always learn from people who are like you, and you can learn from others not like you.

Louie was certainly different.

ONE DOOR CLOSES
AND ANOTHER DOOR OPENS

I N MY FIRST FIVE YEARS IN the TV/appliance business, I refused offers of sales positions with the two largest TV/appliance distributors. One was Igoe Brothers. They sold Kitchen Aid appliances, Dumont TVs, the # 1 brand Fedders room air conditioners, and Andrea TVs. The other was Krich Redisco. They sold the # 1 brand RCA radios, TVs, and the # 1 brand Whirlpool appliances.

I refused to accept the offers of employment because I was already earning more than their top people and was happy with my company. I enjoyed being appreciated for the growth that I was accomplishing. But I did find that every time I told the company's Sales Manager that I was offered a position with another company (but turned it down), I was given a raise in pay.

In 1961, the Zenith distributor, Apollo Distributing Co., called and requested that we meet for a job interview. Richard Slobodien, the son of the owner was their salesman for Passaic County. He recognized how much business I was doing there with my "nothing" Motorola brand with Solly Goldberg at Goldberg's Appliance in Paterson, Harry Hammond at his large store on highway 46 in Lodi, and at Lou Sales in Passaic.

He wanted me on his team. I agreed to go to a meeting after work for another learning experience. I listened politely as they offered me a sales position and surprised them by telling them that I would think about it and let them know. Then, the owner, Dave Slobodien, intervened and said that when they offer a sales position, either the person accepts or the offer is off the table. He said that nobody ever rejected an offer of employment from his company. I said that I was sorry to hear that, but I could not commit. I was at the top of my game with plenty of supporting dealers, with a newly built house and a new mortgage, and two little boys.

The last thing I was looking for was a change. I refused their offer.

Later that same night at 10:30pm, I receive a call from the owner of Cooper Distributing Company, Nate Cooper. He asked if it was true that I had an interview with the Zenith distributor tonight? I told him it was true, but I didn't accept the offer. Then he said. "That distributor is much bigger and their Zenith line is red hot. You'll learn a lot and I'm sure you will do great. I'm going to do you a big favor. You're fired."

"No, Mr. Cooper, I said. I don't want to leave. I want to stay with the company and the territory that I built up in the last 6 years. I'm happy where I am. My dealers love me, and I love them. The business has grown to where we're becoming the leaders."

Nothing I said made a difference; his mind was made up. As of that moment, 10:45pm, I was officially unemployed. I immediately called the sales manager to get my job back. The Sales Manager said that I shouldn't worry and that he would straighten it out with the boss. There must be some misunderstanding.

"We certainly don't want to lose our top man." He said he would call the boss, straighten this out, and call me right back. He did call back to say that the boss was adamant. I was fired, and there was nothing he could do about it.

At 7:00 the next morning, I was unemployed. I called Apollo Distributing to tell them that I had re-considered their offer and decided to accept it.

Bill Wosnitzer, the Sales Manager said, "When can you start?"
"How about right now?" was my answer.
"Good, come over now and let's get started."
It was 7:30 a.m. I was employed again.

1962 Zenith cherrywood color TV.

If You Don't Ask, You Don't Get

MY NEW SALES MANAGER EXPLAINED TO me that my new territory would be Rockland County and Staten Island in New
York, and Northern Bergen County in New Jersey. I was surprised
and disappointed because I had developed so many wonderful relationships with dealers in so many other territories in New Jersey,
but I had no connections in any of these other areas. It would have
been easy to increase business fast with people that I already knew.

The sales manager said, "That's your territory. The decision is
final. We're sure you will do a great job in these areas, even if you
don't know anyone there now."

On my first day, Allen, the former District Sales Manager and
the owner's son-in-law, traveled with me to introduce me to the
dealers in my new territory in Rockland County, NY, which was
just north of northern Bergen County, New Jersey.

The first dealer we saw was on the highway with a small service
and sales store in Suffern, New York. He displayed window signs
for Zenith, Sylvania and Admiral. The first thing the owner told me
was that he had an exclusive arrangement with the Zenith brand
for Rockland County. This dealer said that he was doing very well

selling Zenith, so he could not imagine that there would be any need to make any changes.

I asked, "Why do you display more of the other brands than you do of Zenith since you have an exclusive arrangement with Zenith? He said that he did plenty of business with Zenith, but he makes a lot more money selling the other brands. Naturally, he pushes the other brands because Zenith products sell themselves.

"Everyone comes in and asks for Zenith," he said, "but we all know that there's very little money to be made selling your products. That's why a dealer needs these other brands."

The next week, I came back to Suffern without the previous District Sales Manager, to see if there were other dealers in the area who might be potential accounts.

In the middle of the business district was Suffern Rug & Furniture, located on Main Street, with parking in the rear of the building,. Their window showed signs for all the top brands of TVs, appliances, furniture, rugs, mattresses, and carpets.

I went into the store to explore the possibilities. The salesperson that I spoke to immediately got the owner from his office to speak to me. The owner told me that he had called the Zenith distributor at least six times but had never even received the courtesy of a response.

I told him that I was the new representative and that this was my first week on the job. Then he asked if he could see my book with all the models and prices.

"What do I have to do to get the line?"

I told him there was a problem because the prior salesperson had made an exclusive agreement with another dealer in the area. Since I just started with the company, it would be very difficult to convince my management to make any immediate changes and reverse what the previous salesman had committed to.

I was willing to help him get the line, but I didn't want to make changes that didn't make sense, and that could get me in trouble, especially in only my first week with the distributor. I told him that

I would have to prove to my management that his support would make a real difference for our company in this marketplace. He would need to show a level of commitment, and there would have to be a significant increase in business to justify adding him as a dealer.

He then replied: "How about if I give you an order right now for twenty-five Zenith TVs and some radios? You'll have the biggest display in the area and in my store. Would that do it?" In those days that would be considered a big order.

I thought for a while, and I said, "If you gave me an order for fifty TVs and some radios and commit to have Zenith with the dominant display in your store and agree to have Zenith be your biggest selling brand, then I would try for you." He wrote the order on the spot. If you don't ask, you don't get.

Suffern Rug & Furniture did ten times the volume in Zenith than the other dealer who originally had the exclusive. The other dealer complained, but he never stopped selling the line and never did any less business.

I was recognized that first week as a hero for just doing what made sense and what needed to be done. It's a great feeling to know that you can figure out what is right to do and have the courage to do it. Management was thrilled.

I loved being appreciated. I was hired by Dick Slobodien because he believed in me, and I did just what he expected me to do.

I always believed in the saying: "There are three kinds of people: Those who make things happen. Those who watch things happen. Those who say, 'What happened?'"

I always want to be the person who makes things happen.

HAVE THE GUTS TO MAKE
THE NECESSARY CHANGES

IN 1961, I HAD NEVER BEEN to Staten Island, which was New York City's largest borough in area and smallest in population. This was also part of my new territory.

The Verrazano Bridge connecting Brooklyn to Staten Island was under construction. Families were planning to move from their crowded rental apartments in Brooklyn to suburban residential areas with reasonably priced one-family houses in Staten Island. People could work in Manhattan or Brooklyn and conveniently get to Staten Island with a 30-minute commute by car, instead of an hour of two traveling on the Staten Island Ferry from the St. George Terminal in Staten Island to South Ferry Terminal at the southern tip of Manhattan.

The company's sales manager drove with me on my first day to introduce me to the existing dealers. He told me that on Staten Island, we have an exclusive arrangement to sell only three dealers. He advised me that sales here were excellent.

I was told that the first dealer to see was, by-far, the largest retailer of our Zenith brand. That was New Dorp TV. The store was on a side street of this new and growing residential area with all single-family homes, many recently constructed and many being built.

There was very little parking outside his store. Joe, the owner, looked like the big Mafia don (James Gandolfini) in "The Sopranos" TV series, spoke with a heavy Brooklyn accent, was sloppily dressed, used vulgar street language, and appeared very unprofessional. He looked more like a bouncer in a bar than the owner and salesman for a high-volume store that sold TVs. Joe, his wife, and one salesperson were the only people in the store. Displayed against the walls were about 40 TVs, all in original cartons with the fronts cut out so they could show the TVs live.

Joe lost no time in making it known that he and the two other dealers on Staten Island had the exclusive rights to sell Zenith on Staten Island. His first comment to me was a threat: "If we are going to get along, our exclusive agreement better not change!"

On display were Zeniths, but there were more RCAs. Admirals, Emersons, Olympics and one Sears Kenmore. The reason for the Kenmore was to teach consumers why they shouldn't buy Kenmore by Sears.

I asked him why the Zeniths on display were mostly old models?

His response was "What are you, a smart guy? We make money here. Maybe you don't know it because you are new, but there's very little money in selling Zenith. The big guys in Manhattan kill the prices. Consumers go the Zenith factory showroom at 777 Seventh Ave, pick out what they want, and call us for the pricing. We compete with all the biggest retailers in Manhattan and if we have to, we sell them at little or no profit. Frequently, we can switch them to buy an old model or another brand, and then we can make money.

"We buy all the old Zenith models that we can get because that's where the real money is. I have a special relationship with the ownership of Apollo Distributing, If I ever hear that you added another dealer on Staten Island, I'll stop selling Zenith, and I guarantee you that I will get you fired that same day."

In the car, I asked the Sales Manager if I was really in charge to make any changes with dealers in this territory. His answer was very political. He acknowledged that I had recently made a great move by selling that big dealer in Rockland County, but if he was the salesman in this area, he would never challenge Joe at New Dorp TV.

Next, we visited a long-time service-repair dealer. They also had almost no parking availability. They were a father and his two sons who serviced all brands but sold only Zenith.

Then we went to the Staten Island ferry terminal where thousands of workers every day commuted to and from Manhattan and Brooklyn. They displayed three Zenith TVs, three $250 Zenith Transoceanic radios and six $59.95 Zenith Royal 500 portable radios.

The owner told us that he was one of the directors of a new appliance buying co-operative in Brooklyn called. They stocked and sold many brands of TVs and appliances, including Zenith, which they bought from the New York factory branch.

A year later, my employer authorized me to sell our Zenith line in Brooklyn to Key Buying Co-op. We did volume business with them and with their stores in New York, New Jersey, and the other boroughs of New York City. That was accomplished because the owners of the distributorship convinced the factory that it would be beneficial for everyone. They were right.

In my second week on Staten Island, I drove alone to view the dealers. I saw Staten Island Appliance, a great-looking store on the main street, but it was only one block away from our exclusive dealer. I walked into Staten Island Appliance. The owner was a long-time resident, a local plumbing contractor with a service department and a great reputation for taking care of customers. He had a very nice display of RCA and GE.

The owner, wore a suit and a tie. There was parking in the rear of his store and on the main street in the front of the store. He said that he would love to be able to sell Zenith, "but everyone knows that your company has only three dealers, including the dealer a block away, who they say sells your brand for cost."

I told him that my job was to grow the business and if he could help to make Zenith his major brand and give me a substantial order to show that he was serious about helping to grow our business, that I would try to get him the line.

I knew that the other dealer would scream and try to cause trouble, but I thought that opening up this account with our brand would help—not hurt—our sales. He then gave me a substantial order.

Back at the office, when the sales manager saw the order, he immediately questioned why I would add another dealer in Staten Island, especially a retailer so close to our biggest customer. I reminded him that Joe buys more closeouts than new merchandise. He wasn't helping us to grow the business. I said that if the company supported me here, they would find that we would dramatically increase sales. The company shipped the order.

The next week, the new dealer received their first order. I stopped there the same day as delivery to help him put the models in the prime location in his store and see that everything was set up properly. I did a sales training with him and his people.

Then I went to see our biggest customer in the territory who I knew would be unhappy when he found out what I did.

"Get out of my store," was how the owner greeted me, "You think you won this battle, but it just started. I told you that I would get you fired if you crossed me, and you will be fired today. I already called the owner of the Zenith distributorship. I have a great relationship with him. I am sure that before the day is over, you are going to be out of a job. And that other dealer will never get another piece from Apollo."

That afternoon, I got a call from the sales manager to confirm that the owner received a call from angry Joe, who told the owner that he would stop selling Zenith unless they fired me and that they needed to stop selling the other dealer who had just received the merchandise. He was told that angry dealer was a very important customer, and they would check and get back to him within the hour. The owner and his son discussed the situation, and the son returned his call and told Joe that we had made a terrible mistake, but with advice from their lawyers, it would be illegal to stop selling that other dealer who already had the merchandise on display. They told him they would see what they could do about finding some old models to sell him at special prices.

I had been hired because the son of the owner believed that I had the guts to make changes and that changes were needed to grow the business. I had done exactly what he was looking for me to do. The sales manager asked me what I thought would happen next. I told him not to worry, and that this was just the first step towards making this territory a really good Zenith territory.

The big close-out dealer never stopped selling our products, never did less business, and still bought as many old models as he could get.

The new business-like dealer—with parking in the rear of his store and on the main street in front of the store—did almost as much business as Joe had done with the close-out and new models. A win for our side.

Train, Support and Appreciate Service People

RCA—Radio Corporation of America—was founded in 1919. David Sarnoff was the first general manager. From 1930 to 1965 he was the president. RCA created the first nationwide American radio network—the National Broadcasting Company (NBC)—and was a pioneer in the introduction of black-and-white TVs and, later, color TVs.

RCA was the largest manufacturer of TVs and provided service with their own RCA Service Company. They had all new service trucks with great signage and well trained, uniform-wearing service techs. They advertised their service on their NBC network and they were growing.

I didn't believe that the independent TV servicers understood the threat of being eliminated by RCA. Someone needed to tell them, I decided that would be me.

Our distributorship had its own service department to support the independent dealers. Although we had a service department, the TV service was done by independent authorized service agencies that were paid by Zenith Radio Corp out of Chicago.

I arranged to have service-training meetings for all the

independent TV service agencies in order to gain their support. I set up a 7:00 a.m. breakfast meeting for all TV service agencies and service people at a local hotel so it wouldn't interfere with their making money for the day. We had lunch meetings, too.

I would start with a thank you.

"Welcome, we appreciate that you have given us your time to listen and learn. I hope you all understand that you and our Zenith company are in the fight of our lives to survive. RCA wants to put you—the independent service companies—out of business and put Zenith out of business. too.

"RCA uses those new printed boards which you guys are constantly asked to fix. Zenith uses the good, old fashioned wiring which you guys have told us has always been reliable, easier to fix, and that there is no reason to change. We listened to you and didn't change. We appreciate you and what you do for the consumers.

"Now it's time for you to tell your customers to trust their **INDEPENDENT SERVICE AGENCIES** and tell all the consumers to buy Zenith—the better brand—and not to buy RCA, the brand that is trying to put you out of business."

All of our guests received the latest spec books of technical information about our products. After they ate their breakfast, our service manager would go over all the new information about our Zenith TV technical data.

"Our distributorship is always here to help you," I . Just call our Service Manager any time. Telephone number is 973-228-5000

I told them that service technicians were Zenith's best supporters because they understood that wired circuitry is the best and easiest to repair, compared to the new printed circuitry that RCA uses exclusively in their TVs.

I told them that the RCA Service Company is expanding the RCA service business and trying to put YOU, the independent service agencies out of business. You should fight back and tell all your service customers to buy Zenith and not to buy RCA because you know it is the better brand that will last longer and require less service.

Then I would introduce our friendly service manager, who reviewed the technical information and gave each technician the technical brochures and a gift. Then came question-and-answer time.

It worked! The independent servicers became our best supporters.

Even the ones who didn't sell TVs all told their customers to buy Zenith and not to buy RCA.

FIND A RETAILER THAT HAS PLENTY OF WELL-LIGHTED PARKING SO THAT CUSTOMERS FEEL SAFE SHOPPING AT NIGHT

CASTLETON AVENUE AND RICHMOND AVENUE, THE location of, was a residential area in the western section of Staten Island. Similar to a Radio Shack, Staten Island Radio Hospital sold radio and electronics parts, small TV tubes, and picture tubes to do-it yourself enthusiasts. The didn't sell TVs. I spoke to the owner, John McGillivray, who was a hard-working go-getter from Canada, who lived in a house next to the store, with his wife and children and his brother-in-law.

The store had a very large lighted parking area. Parking was an important feature because consumers appreciated having good parking. They felt comfortable shopping there at night.-

Staten Island Radio Hospital expanded their Zenith-only sales to eventually become my showcase store, displaying 20 different Zenith models. Because the factory couldn't keep up with the demand in 1962-1965, there were shortages. Merchandise was allocated to the different distributors.

John helped us grow the business. For years, his store displayed a large sign in the front windows that said: "LARGEST DISPLAY OF ZENITH TVs IN NEW YORK." In the *Staten Island Advance* newspaper, they advertised the same message. The Zenith factory showroom at 777 Seventh Ave in Manhattan could show but not sell any Zenith products. The Staten Island showroom could sell the products and deliver the next day if they could get the product. They got the Zenith products.

Staten Island Radio Hospital sold the features, benefits, and quality of the brand, not just price. They explained to consumers that low prices mean nothing if the retailer does not have the product to deliver.

Staten Island Radio Hospital delivered either on the day of purchase or the next day. They made sales to consumers miles away, who were waiting for. Because they had the merchandise (or something similar) to deliver, they became the go-to location for Zenith to see, learn, buy, and get fast delivery. Having only one brand helps profitability, too. And having a well-lighted safe parking lot with plenty of parking spaces allowed consumers to come and buy at night. That helped, too.

Another exclusive dealer that I established was in the Stapleton section of Staten Island. He was a TV serviceman with a small store, but with a big following of mostly Italian service customers. I put him in the selling business, too. I set him up with a bank floor plan because he didn't have enough money.

He loved the sense of importance he got from being a big retailer and service center with the top national brand.

His girlfriend, Rose, did most of the selling and she was great. Together, they kept the store open seven days a week because they enjoyed their success so much. I recommended that they advertise big ads in the *Staten Island Advance* and I created the ads for him. He sold only Zenith. The proudest day of his life was when he drove his brand-new Cadillac to the store and parked it right in front so everyone would know what he had been able to achieve.

I was happy for him and proud of what he accomplished. He helped us to grow our business.

Another exclusive dealer that I set up was in the Tottenville area on the southern end of the island opposite Perth Amboy, NJ. I researched this rural area and found there was one appliance dealer that we were already selling and one hardware store that sold vacuum cleaners.

I franchised the hardware store to sell our Zenith TVs. Their 21-year-old salesclerk was a young man who was anxious to learn the business. He became a great salesman. He was loved by his customers and he enjoyed selling so much, that after about a year, he opened his own store in the same area, with the blessing of the hardware store owner, to sell only Zenith TVs and Maytag appliances. He did a great job of advertising with flyers every week and sales once a month at night which was the Maytag way in those days. That helped him (and us) grow even more.

In 1967, five years after I had started, I was selling to all twenty television retailers in Staten Island. Six of them sold Zenith exclusively. Obviously, business was good.

In 1966, the Zenith National convention was held at the Statler Hilton Hotel in Chicago. Zenith president Len Truesdell congratulated Apollo ownership for being the top Zenith distributor in the country. He added that Apollo has accomplished an unbelieve feat by having a BPI of 51 percent in one of their New York boroughs. That means 51 percent of all TV sales for 1966 were with the Zenith brand. That was the first time it had ever been done and still the last time it has been done. That was our Staten Island territory.

CREATE SPECIAL MOMENTS
WITH YOUR CUSTOMERS

MARTY FRIEDMAN WAS THE TOP SALESPERSON at Apollo and enjoyed a friendship with Dick Slobodein, the son of the owner. I had heard people say that Dick was heartless impatient, and demanding. The truth was that he wanted results. The salespeople were well-treated and well-paid, but he demanded effort and results. Each year he would replace one or two of the eight salespeople who had turned in the worst sales performance. It wasn't about personalities; he was doing what he felt was necessary to grow the business. The company was recognized as the best Zenith distributor in the country for each of the six years that I was there.

In 1965, Jim Frangos, one of our district sales managers, had the smallest sales area. Jim lived near Princeton University. He dressed and spoke and acted like he was a professor at an Ivy League school. He influenced me to dress like he did.

Dick Slobodein offered Jim additional territory so he could expand the business and make more money. Jim refused, saying that he enjoyed having a small territory, selling fewer retailers. He was happy making the money he was making.

Dick told him that if he didn't accept the new territory, he would be fired. Jim left the company. He was out of a job for a year, until he convinced the famous Madison Square Garden in New York City to hire him as the National Sales Manager.

I visited Jim in his new office on the top floor of the Garden where the executive offices were located. His job was to book all events into the arena except pro sports; events like the Ringling Brothers Circus, concerts, prizefights, and other sporting events.

At that time, the New York Knicks were the hottest basketball team. Tickets were impossible to get. They were tearing up the courts with players like Willis Reed, Walt Frazier, Dave DeBusschere, Bill Bradley, Earl Monroe, and Phil Jackson. Having been a fan of the game all my life, I asked Jim if he could get me a couple of season seats to the sold-out Garden. He did. He even introduced me to his friend Sy who was the maître d' at their private club restaurant, the Penn Plaza Club, on the top floor of the Garden.

Jim told me that he arranged for Dick Slobodien to buy the Red Holzman season tickets that were at the players' entry to the court in the second row. At the time, Red Holzman was the Knicks' coach and general manager.

It must have cost Dick a fortune to get those seats, but whatever the price, they were worth it. I frequently went to the games with Dick and customers, who were always impressed. I was a lucky guy.

In addition to the game itself, celebrities were always sitting next to us or in the first row just below us, adding to the experience. Dick often gave me the tickets to use with customers.

We would have dinner at the Penn Plaza Club, then sit in the best seats in the house and watch the game, surrounded by celebrities. Those were exciting times. I even had my own parking spot directly across the street at the Madison Square Garden Garage.

I learned a lot at Apollo. Every year, Zenith had their Annual Distributor Meeting in the Main Ballroom at the Statler Hilton Hotel in Chicago.

Dick would invite me to attend a private dinner with his father,

Dave; the Zenith national sales manager, and the Zenith order clerk. Business was so good that merchandise was always in short supply. Merchandise was allocated by the head order clerk who always attended our dinner and managed to favor us when allocating the back orders.

Our dinner reservation was usually at 7:00 o'clock at the Cape Cod Room in the Drake Hotel. When we arrived, there were always 50 or more people, all with 6:30 and 7:00 p.m. reservations, waiting to get in. The crowd would extend out into the hallway and to the street. Someone from our group would wave to Patrick Braden, the maître d', at the front of the line, and he would always say in a loud voice; "Please, let Mr. Slobodien and his party in. Right this way Mr. Slobodien." Dave knew how to take good care of all the right people and Dave always got what he wanted.

It was another lesson that I enjoyed learning.

The Cape Cod Room at the Drake Hotel had a well-deserved reputation for the finest seafood and service in Chicago. They boasted that they were the largest sellers of turbot fish and that it was "flown in daily from the Mediterranean." They were also famous for their Philadelphia Bookbinder soup with sherry. At that time, when a first-class stamp was four cents and gasoline sold for about thirty cents a gallon, the platters for our table had lobster, stone crabs, shrimp, caviar, and crabmeat and probably cost $150 a person, but Dave spared no expense. They served only the best wines and liquors. The guests included one important retailer. Everyone loved it.

Of course, I loved it, too, and from that experience, I learned to enjoy those special moments and I still use them to build relationships with others.

Ever since then, whenever I have visited Chicago for the trade conventions, [maybe 40+ times] I always included one or two nights for dinner with customers at the Cape Cod Room. In 2014, I went there and Patrick Braden was there, but only part time. At that time, he told my guests that Marty Friedman was his oldest regular customer. I had given him the $50. in the afternoon before dinner. That is the entry fee that Dave taught me.

It was well worth the price.

In 1967 with Dick's policy of having me train the newest sales-people for one day. That's when I met Irv Needle, our newest sales-man. Dick believed that I would help set a good example of how the job should be done, so each "newbie" would accompany me to see how I worked with my accounts.

I would always pick them up at their home at 7 a.m., which was unusual for them because most wholesale salespeople begin their day much later.

My workday started with seeing a retailer at 7:30 a.m. or 8:00 am and seeing my last dealer at 7pm.

One day, after spending the day with our newest hire, he said something that I had never heard before.

He said that he liked everything he saw and appreciated my help, advice, and support. Then, he offered to do me a big favor and tell me how I could make much more money than I was currently making. He said that I had all the right contacts and tools to do what he was about to recommend. I thanked him, but said imme-diately that it wasn't possible for me to make more money because I was already the top earner in the company, and in the business, and that I was very happy with my present situation.

He went on to explain that several years earlier he was the first independent sales representative company for Sony TVs & radios in the NY/NJ area. For the five years on that job, he claimed he made more money than he could ever make as a distributor salesperson because he was paid 5 percent on all sales. He said that I was prob-ably making 1 percent and 5 percent is better than 1 percent. At that time, my compensation was about 1%. Now I was listening.

When Sony made the decision to hire their own sales man-ager and sales force, they ended their agreement with Irv. He then found a transistor radio manufacturer from Taiwan and became their independent sales representative company. That arrangement lasted for three or four years and, again, he made "tons of money" working for 4 percent instead of 1 percent that he might make working for a distributor.

Having seen my sales ability, the network and rapport I had built up with dealers in the region, Irv insisted that such a move for me "could not miss."

He was adamant that all I had to do would be to contact different Japanese and Asian manufacturers and all sales managers from companies I knew. Tell them that I was going to open my own new sales rep agency to sell TVs, electronics, and appliances. I thought about it and decided that it was worth a try. I wrote and called Hitachi, Toshiba, Sanyo, Sony, Aiwa (pronounced EYE WAH), Panasonic, Mitsubishi, Sharp, and anyone else that I could think of. I contacted the sales managers that I knew and had known seeking their help.

Within a month, I had an agreement to represent Aiwa (Japan), Andrea Radio Corp. (Long Island City, NY), and Telex Phenol (Chicago); and I had a handshake agreement from George Stewart, the VP of Toshiba, that in six months I would be their sales rep for New York and New Jersey.

Dick and I had been friends for six years. He taught me a lot about the business. I accompanied him on trips where he took no other salespeople.

We enjoyed each other's company and ideas. We regularly went out together with our wives. When I told him I was leaving to become an independent sales rep, he said that I must be under too much pressure. He suggested that I take a couple of weeks off and go on vacation. The company would pay for it. If it were a matter of money, we could discuss it, although I was already their highest paid employee. He reminded me nobody had ever left Apollo voluntarily. I told him I would think about it overnight. The next day, I told Dick it was a difficult decision, but I was leaving.

"You know, I like you. We have a special relationship," Dick told me. "But if you leave now, I guarantee you will never be allowed to come back."

It was a tremendous leap of faith, to face unemployment again, but I was ready take a chance at even greater success. Years later, until his death, Dick and I remained friends and would see each other a few times a year.

An Agreement is Only as Good
as the Other Person's Intent

Andrea Radio Corporation in Long Island City was founded in 1934 by Frank Angelo D'Andrea, Sr. He was a radio and TV pioneer who had worked in Italy for Guglielmo Marconi, the inventor of long-distance radio transmission. In 1909, Marconi won the Nobel Prize in Physics, in recognition of his contribution to the development of wireless telegraphy.

Starting in 1947, D'Andrea made TVs in Long Island City, NY. In 1961, the company developed and produced the audio center for the first manned space capsule, Project Mercury, which carried astronaut Alan Shepherd into space.

Although the Andrea people said that a contract between us was not necessary, I still had my attorney draw up an agreement before I accepted joining them as their exclusive sales agency for NY/NJ. They hesitatingly agreed to everything that I said that I needed to succeed.

The year was 1967. The agreement was notarized and signed by the president, Frank A. D'Andrea, Jr., their executive vice-president and me.

As part of the terms in the agreement, Andrea agreed to pay

for my office, my showroom, a service truck, parts, and a service technician for my new company.

The KitchenAid and Fedders distributor previously sold the Andrea TVs. He apparently had resigned the line because there was no demand for the brand.

I decided that the best way to introduce the change in distribution was to host a private event. Andrea agreed to pay for that too. I selected the Main Ballroom at the new Suburban Hotel in East Orange. Andrea sent the models for display. I sent out invitations that read: "Dinner, drinks, and meet Frank D'Andrea, Jr. and Camille D'Andrea. See the new Andrea TVs for 1968."

Northern New Jersey has historically had a large Italian population and many went into the business of servicing and selling TVs. This was an opportunity to show these dealers how they could make more profit with this brand and meet and support a famous family of an Italian manufacturer of TVs.

I was right. The Italian retailers came to the show. Angelo & his wife from Angelo's TV in Newark; Bess and Joe Napolitano from Keystone Appliance in North Bergen and many more. They were thrilled to talk mostly in Italian to the owners of the TV manufacturer most of the time during my presentation and during dinner. They all pledged their support to the company and the brand.

Dealers love to meet with "big people." During the show and afterwards, they called other dealers and encouraged them to buy and support the Andrea brand. The show was a huge success, not only in writing orders, but also in quickly getting us off on the right foot with the dealers. Andrea could see we could do things for them that nobody else had ever done before. The former GM from Igoe Brothers was Gus Damato who was of Italian descent which was probably the reason that he took on the line originally.

I had been advised, correctly, that my experience and talent was perfect for me to be an independent entrepreneur. As an independent sales agency with an exclusive territory, I made more money the first week and the first month and the first year than I ever made as a top salesperson for the distributor.

1966: Marketing East's first brand as a sales Agency for Andrea Radio & TV with $2, 500 Theatre-in-the-Round that Marty sold to Bloomingdales.

My wife was a big help, with her previous experience working for the top small appliance distributor in NJ when she was in high school. We had a tiny office in Union when we started and she was in charge. That freed me up to concentrate on sales. I hired my first salesman, Tom, who previously worked for Frigidaire. We added Andrea dealers, like Huffman & Boyle, the largest furniture chain in New Jersey. They loved selling our $2,500 beautiful Theatre-in-the-Round TV/radio/phonograph unit. Then we added Bloomingdale's Department stores and Alexanders Department stores, and Holtzhousen's Dept store in Jersey City. Soon I was able to add another salesman. I always believed that you have to make investments to grow.

After many months of good selling, I noticed that Andrea had not approved any of my choices for either my proposed showroom location that they agreed to pay for, or for the parts, salesman, or truck. They also had not found the service technician that they had agreed to hire.

Andrea TV billboard was a thank you to Pete Moraha
for recommending me to be their sales agent.

When I asked my attorney about our signed agreement, he said that an agreement is only as good as the word of the people who sign it. It seemed I was learning yet another lesson the hard way. Apparently, they never planned to pay for what they were agreeing to. But since it was the only way to get me to get started, they signed the agreement. And it worked.

My attorney told me that if I needed Andrea to make a living, I should not sue them, so I did not. I stayed and grew their business. Five years later, I resigned their line after my business had grown with their brand and with other brands. By that time, Andrea had stopped investing in developing any new models. Years later, I found that I had never deposited my last commission check for about $20,000. It had been in my office drawer all that time.

I called Andrea and visited the factory in Long Island City, one last time to get a replacement check. They knew that it had not been deposited and never called because they believed I was holding it pending a future lawsuit. They knew that I would win if I did sue them.

My son Craig's advice was: "We are not in the suing business. We are in the selling business."

KEEP SUCCEEDING AT
WHAT YOU KNOW HOW TO DO

M Y SECOND PRODUCT LINE WAS THE Aiwa tape recorder company from Japan.

Someone in Germany invented tape recorders during World
War II. They shared their invention with their war partner, Japan.
After the war in 1947, Mr. Ikegeri claimed to develop the Ikegeri
tape recording head that was needed to operate small tape recorders. He gave the new technology to his brother who started the first
tape recorder company in Japan: Aiwa.

In 1963 Phillips Electronics introduced the popular compact
cassette recorder at the International Show in Berlin, which grew
in popularity because of its small size and easy use.

In the USA Alexander M. Poniatoff, an American soldier, found
a German tape recorder in Germany after the war was over. He
brought it back to the USA and became one the first tape recorder
manufacturers. He named his company Ampex, which represented
his first three initials.

In 1964, Aiwa introduced the model TP707, which was their
first portable compact cassette recorder. The former sales manager
of International Harvester freezers recommended me to Aiwa and

I contacted them. Their USA importer was located in Chicago. I phoned the sales manager, offering to represent their brand in New Jersey. With his approval, I flew to Chicago to meet with them.

They had a factory branch for New Yorke with five salespeople, but most of their sales were in New York. They did little business in New Jersey.

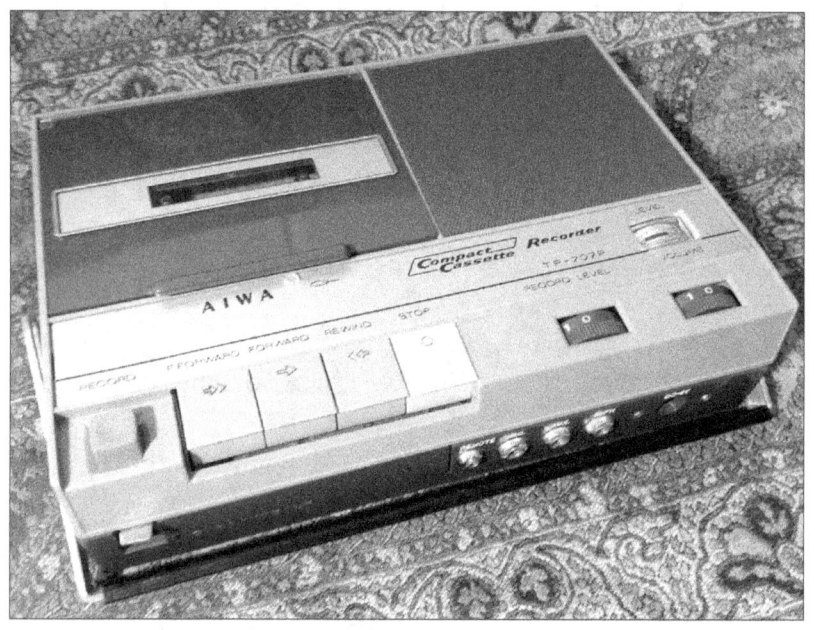

1967 Aiwa TP707.

They agreed to have Marketing East be their New Jersey sales agency. Bernie Buchwald, the sales manager, said that he would help me get started and agreed to come to New Jersey for a few days to help me get started.

He asked me to make three appointments for the first day with the three biggest accounts. He said that he would sell all three. I didn't believe that he or anyone could do that, but I was certainly willing to learn. I made the appointments.

I picked him up at Newark Airport at 8;00 a.m. Bernie was an impeccably dressed. He was a 70-year-old man, balding, with white hair. Just to confirm that the buyer didn't forget our appointment,

I called the buyer from the Prince Range company [10 stores] to reconfirm our appointment with the sales manager of Aiwa, and that we would be on time for our 9:00 a.m. appointment with him.

He confirmed the meeting, but he told me that he could not buy anything right now because he had too much inventory of other brands. He said that this would be just a short courtesy meeting.

Prince Range was the largest retailer of TVs, radios, and appliances in New Jersey, with ten leased departments located in discount department stores. We meet with the buyer, who was also the son-in-law of the owner.

Ed Israel of Newark Bamberger Gets Merchandising Award

Jack Mikulski (left), National Sales Manager for Aiwa/Selectron presents the company's Distinguished Merchandising Award to Edward Israel (center), Radio Department Buyer for Bambergers-New Jersey. Looking on is Marty Friedman of M. Friedman Associates, Inc., New Jersey representatives for Aiwa. The award represents recognition of the store's efforts to promote the growth and sales of the tape recorder industry through innovations, advertising, and promotional activities.

1970: Bamberger's NJ Award from AIWA.

Before we started, the buyer told Bernie and me, that this was just a courtesy visit. He could not buy anything because he was overstocked and had to move out existing merchandise before there would be any more buying. The Aiwa sales manager said that he understood that and appreciated Roy's honesty.

By 1967, technology and volume production had driven the portable radio prices down. Small transistor radios were now coming from Hong Kong, and Taiwan. This new category was a very high-volume business. Ten million radios sold in the USA in 1967.

From his big bag, Bernie Buchwald, took out a small portable transistor radio, a mid-sized one, and a large FM/AM/shortwave portable model. He said that these were not current models, just closeouts. He asked if Prince Range ever buys closeouts. "If the price is right," Roy said cautiously, we buy quantities of close-outs."

"Good," said Bernie, glancing at the notes in his sales book. "We have 567 of the medium-size model. Your price . . ." then he paused. He looked like he was trying hard to get a crazy price for this customer . . ."is $8.47." I thought it looked like a model that should sell for about $40 at retail. Then Bernie said, "We have 952 of the second, smaller model." Again, he hesitated, looking at his notes. Then he mumbled, "Let's get rid of them all! They would cost you $5.50 each."

I was still just watching quietly, but a model like the one he was holding would probably sell at retail for at least $30.

By this time, I could see that Roy's interest was piqued. He asked, "And what about the third model?" The third model was the large portable/electric FM/AM/Shortwave transistor radio. Bernie looked thoughtfully at his notes again, and then said, "I have to get rid of all 237 units. Your cost would be $22 each." It was probably a $70 retail item. Without hesitation, Roy said, "I'll take them all."

"Okay," was all Bernie said without batting an eye. He was completely nonchalant. If he were surprised at all by Roy's reversal on his buying position, he didn't show it. I simply sat there in silent disbelief.

Then Bernie opened up a heavily insulated box that had recently been air freighted from Japan with all the air freight tags on it. Inside was a portable, state-of-the-art, high-fidelity, battery and electric reel-to-reel tape recorder in a white plastic case with a lock. It had the shape and size of a business briefcase including a white handle. There had never been anything like it on the market.

Bernie announced that he recently received this item from Japan, and he showed it so far to only one customer, the General Manager and Buyer from Dayton Hudson Department Stores [later Target stores] in Minneapolis. They were one of the biggest electronics retailers in the country at that time. "I made a deal with them to be the first to advertise this item for their stores in the West."

Then he plugged it into an outlet and demonstrated it for Roy, recording his sales presentation on the recorder. The quality was the best that Roy or I had ever heard on a tape recorder. Roy had only one question: "How much?"

Bernie said that it would cost Prince Range $140 but he needed an agreement that it would not be sold for less than $199. But first he needed to know that he had the right partner to introduce this new product into the marketplace in the New York area and participate with their Aiwa co-op advertising program.

Roy said, "Don't look any further. That's for me. How many do I have to buy to be your guy in this market?" Bernie said that Roy could be our guy, but he didn't want him to over-extend himself.

"Just buy enough for each of your ten stores to show them on display, with enough back-up for the first ad." Initially, there will be limited quantities, but if Roy wanted to partner with us, Bernie promised to make sure that he would get what he wanted.

Then Bernie took out a small Aiwa model TP32 reel-to-reel tape recorder that sold for $24.95; a step-up new cassette recorder, model TP707, that sold for about $49.95; and the more featured model that sold for $69.95. At that, Roy backed away saying he could not justify buying those models because he already had too many like them from Panasonic, Hitachi, and GE.

Bernie said that he understood, but that he couldn't sell just closeouts and the newest model to someone who wasn't a serious customer. He suggested that Roy buy just one of each of the tape recorder models for display in each store, with three units to back them up in his ten stores. That would "show that you are a genuine account. Obviously, if you are not willing to do that, I just can't give you the other units."

Roy thought and thought. Then he said, "You sold me. I will give you the orders for all categories."

I was shocked. Roy wrote the orders and we left. When we got back in my car, Bernie asked, "Now, who is the next customer?" I thought, he must be kidding, but I started driving.

Our next appointment was with the buyer for L. Bamberger & Co, the largest department store chain in New Jersey and the heaviest print advertiser. Their headquarters was in Newark. They had ten major department stores throughout the state. About twenty years later they would be acquired and re-branded to be Macy's and the Bamberger's name would be retired to the retailing graveyard. They were not only my most prestigious account, but from a practical sense they were a volume seller of consumer electronics, TVs, and appliances.

Bernie began to tell the buyer exactly the same story that he had told the buyer at Prince Range. By the time Bernie was through, Ed bought all three categories, although not many close-out radios.

Then we went to Paterson, to speak to a company that had leased electronics departments in 50 discount stores throughout the country. The buyer bought the same merchandise that we had sold to the other two dealers.

Later that night over dinner, I asked Bernie how he could deliver the same closeout radios to all three accounts, and how he could allow each of the three to be the first to advertise the newest state-of-the-art product. He gave me a look and said, "Do you think that we could have made any sales if we just tried to sell them the regular merchandise? They all started out telling you the answer was NO. You have a lot to learn, kid. Sometimes you have to do things to get a new prospect's attention. They can never appreciate what you can do for them and what the other guys can't do until they become customers."

I have never believed in that kind of selling, but in this case, maybe he was right. Surely, he had put me on the fast track to be the high-volume sales rep in the area for portable recorders.

Initially, the three dealers received only the tape recorders and cassette recorders and some of the closeout radios; none of that new portable reel-to-reel tape recorder. The model they had seen was a prototype that didn't get delivered until about six months later., and then with a serious price increase it was taken off the market. When the closeout radios were gone Bernie substituted other models of similar value.

At first, they were all furious, but that passed because they found that the Aiwa recorders were outselling all other brands of recorders, probably because we were the only sales reps to visit and train their retail salespeople. All three accounts were very happy in the end and continued to do more business with us.

Within two years the New Jersey territory with three salespeople was producing the same volume of sales as the entire New York territory with their five salespeople. Then Bernie decided to close the New York branch and give me that territory too. I hired one of their salespeople and that helped us grow the business more than double.

Although I might not have always agreed with his methods, I always had a good time with Bernie and respected his knowledge and ability. For years, we did business together with Aiwa and later with other brands when he became the sales manager for another brand. He became my mentor.

One of the brands was one of Japan's largest financial companies with their radios, tape recorders, etc. Their name was Marubeni Iida.

How can you call all that work? It was fun.

Everything You Learn
Could Come in Handy Some Day

OUR AIWA BUSINESS BOOMED. ONE OF my secrets was that my salesmen and I visited every store, put batteries in all the display models, and recorded a sales presentation on every recorder. None of the other brands did that.

Since the retail salespeople didn't know how to operate the new recorders, and they didn't want to embarrass themselves, they didn't put batteries in the units. To overcome that, I would show them exactly how to make a recording on each machine: "Hold these two buttons down [record and play] like this . . . the machine is recording now." I would say: "This is the Aiwa compact cassette recorder from Japan that I am recording on now. Aiwa is the largest selling brand because it has the clearest sound and is easiest to use. The regular price here at Bamberger's is $69.95, but today it is on sale with a savings of $20. for only $49.95. It is very popular for the high school or college students who want to improve their grades using an easy tool to memorize and learn. Now push the Stop Key and see the recording STOP. Push the REWIND button and see the tape rewind and STOP AT THE BEGINNING. Now push the button Play to see Recorder PLAY again."

All the salespeople had to do to demonstrate the units was to push the play button on the model and hear me say: "You are listening to the new Aiwa tape recorder, model TP707. Aiwa tape recorders are made in Japan and they are the largest manufacturer of tape recorders. This is the best-selling tape recorder in the world because it has the best sound, is the easiest to operate, and it is on sale now at all L. Bamberger & Co. stores. The regular price is $69.95, but it is on sale today with a savings of $20. You can buy it today for your student so they can get better grades, for only $49.95. It is a great tool for students because the Aiwa tape recorder makes it easier to learn and remember what you learned. It's the best way to improve their grades in high school and in college."

Then the salesperson would push the rewind button to have the unit rewind and be ready to start at the beginning again. Fortunately, none of my competitors did what I did to make sales. That effort sold AIWA recorders for many years. Thirty years later, at conventions and sales meetings, dealers would tell me that they still use my tapes to sell their tape recorders!

All the courses that I had taken at Fairleigh Dickinson in voice, diction, and public speaking had paid off.

Old Timers in the business have told me that I made the difference in selling AIWA. Years later customers were still listening to my voice telling them the story of "Why to buy the Aiwa."

SUCCESS HELPS TO BUILD
ON MORE SUCCESS

M Y SALES REP COMPANY SOLD ANDREA TVs, Aiwa recorders, radios, small TVs, and Telex Phonola phonographs, and five or six other electronics brands. Eventually, we added Precor, a very strong transistor-radio line from Hong Kong.

Because the big volume buying offices were in New York, we moved our office to midtown Manhattan. I found a low-cost co-op office at Two Penn Plaza above Madison Square Garden at Seventh Avenue and 33rd Street. The co-op office gave me a telephone number, an answering service with a receptionist, conference rooms, and a dozen desks with telephones.

In 1968, I read in the trade newspaper *Home Furnishings Daily* about a sales rep company in California called Marketing West. The name said something, and I liked it. I decided to change my company name to Marketing East Industries Corp., which sounded much more official than Marty Friedman Associates.

A friend of mine was creative director at Cunningham & Walsh, a major Madison Avenue advertising agency. He was the person who created the Folger coffee ads for Proctor & Gamble and created an iconic TV ad for Chiffon Margarine. The premise

of the ad was that the margarine tasted like real butter. In the commercial, Chiffon Margarine fooled Mother Nature into thinking it
was really butter, not a substitute. Mother Nature became "angry"
at the discovery, summoned some thunder and lightning, and said
the famous tagline, "It's not nice to fool Mother Nature."

My friend designed my new logo and a business card based
on the new name. I loved that it had the feel and presence of a big
company: Marty Friedman, President, Marketing East Industries
Corp., Two Penn Plaza, New York, NY 10001; 212-878-3000.

From 1965 to 1986, we sold to all of the large retailers in New
York: Macy's, Abraham & Strauss, Alexander's, S. Klein, J. C.
Penney, Gimbel's, Sam Goody, E.J. Korvettes, F.W. Woolworth Co,
and P.C. Richard & Son.

In New Jersey we did business with: Bamberger's, Two Guys,
Channel Lumber, Rickel Home Centers, Grandway, S.E. Nichols,
Brick Church, and many others.

In New England our clients included: Caldor, Ann & Hope, Apex,
Zayre's, Lechmere, Jordan Marsh, Somerville Lumber, and Bradlees.

We frequently introduced new product categories and taught
retailers how to sell them, including: Sanyo microwave ovens, the
American Food Processor, Ampex, video cassettes, kerosene heaters, Ian Jones International Computers (unassembled), Telematch
TV games, Southwestern Bell Telephones (when consumers could
finally own their own phones), Freedom Phones (the first portable
telephone), Omron pocket calculators, Bearcat scanners, Numark
telephone answering machines, Uniden car radar detectors, eight
track tapes, compact discs and players.

In 1967 Only three manufacturers made and sold kitchen ventilation. I started selling Rangaire from Cleburne, TX as their sales
rep in 1967. They manufactured three models of chest freezers and
$99 range hoods. Their current reps were electronics people who
didn't know appliance retailers or how to sell appliances.

In my first week trying to sell their chest freezers, I contacted
NATM, which was (and still is) a buying cooperative of eight major

appliance retailers with multiple stores nationally. I agreed to make a presentation to their buyers of the three models of chest freezers at their semi-annual meeting at a hotel in Baltimore. I showed them the models and answered questions. They liked the fact that the brand was not well known and the prices were lower than Frigidaire and GA.

CORDLESS $50 OFF

FREEDOM PHONE® WITH MEMORY & 1500 FT. RANGE

INTRODUCTORY SALE $189
$239 after July 14

Stay outside this summer and keep in touch with Freedom Phone®, the new fully-featured cordless telephone from Southwestern Bell. Save $50 now through July 14 during our introductory sale.

• Conservations come in clearly up to 1500' from the base
• Coiled antenna design provides more surface, better reception
• Tone/pulse switchable for use with MCI® or Sprint®
• Memory automatically dials 3 most often called numbers
• Convenient last number redial saves you time
• Personal security code protects against unauthorized access to your line
• Set the ringer volume control as loud or as low as you like
• Batteries in handset (included) charge quickly and have extended life so you can use the phone more, recharge less
• AC cord for base also included
• Model 4000X†

Freedom Phone, state-of-the-art at that time.

They gave me purchase orders for truckloads of their chest freezers to ship to their stores all over the USA.

A month later, the U.S. government changed the energy requirements for freezers, requiring them to be more energy efficient. Rangaire decided to stop manufacturing freezers. It could have been a very short relationship because I knew that appliance retailers would not be interested in selling $100 items because their salespeople could not make enough money for the value of their time.

I told them good bye. They told me that they would like to pay for me to fly to Texas first class, stay in a nice hotel, play golf for a couple of days, and discuss how to make range hoods profitable to sell to appliance retailers.

At that time, the two big manufacturers were Broan for inexpensive range hoods, and Vent-A-Hood for higher-priced range hoods.

Consumers didn't understand the purpose for kitchen ventilation, which is the reason that so much of the business was with inexpensive Broan models that were sold to builders, home centers, and hardware stores.

The VP of Engineering at Rangaire explained to me that the reasons for buying a "properly designed, powerful range hood" are:

They can remove cooking grease. The average kitchen produces 1 lb. per year into the kitchen. Where does it go?

1. They remove carbon monoxide and carbon dioxide that come from gas burners. You don't want those fumes to be breathed in by your children.

2. They remove steam and water vapor that can crack the wood cabinets in your kitchen

3. They remove cooking odors from the kitchen that can go into the rest of the house

4. They provide light above the cooking area to see better

5. Inexpensive range hoods made too much noise and don't filter out the grease

An effective range hood needs to move air and contaminants with at least 400 CFM (Cubic Feet per Minute) extraction or more, in order to be effective in an average kitchen. Since Broan range hoods at that time were listed at 190 CFM, and Rangaire was listed at 200 CFM, neither one could do an effective job.

After two fun days of golf with their executives, we sat down to learn why people should buy kitchen ventilation. Then I proposed a marketing plan which provided a good profit for the dealers to sell their products. They accepted my plan.

One 40-inch-wide wood display was needed, with five models hooked up live with the lowest-, priced model on the bottom. A price tag on every model with model number, original cost, cost savings, net cost to consumer, and key features and benefits, plus the words "Lowest Price Guaranteed"

The Header on the display said RANGAIRE.

On the bottom $99 with original price $129

Next above at $149.98 with original price $199

Next above at $199.98 with original price $249

Next above at $249.98 with original price $299

Next above at $299.98 with original price $399

A header above with the Rangaire logo and script below:

"Protect your families health with a properly sized range hood."

Retail sales incentives would be paid by the Rangaire Company

It was so successful that within a year they recommended the program for all their sales rep territories in the country.

Rangaire sales grew. Fifteen years later, when our sales in the New York area finally equaled Broan's sales, Nortek (the parent company of Broan) bought Rangaire for millions of dollars, hired Fred Rogers, who was the former sales manager of Rangaire and fired Marketing East.

Fred said that felt badly because of our long relationship and the great job we had done for them, but Broan management ordered him to fire us because they believed that they didn't need our sales help anymore. After all, they now owned most of the business.

Six months later, we were enlisted as the sales representatives for Nutone range hoods and intercoms. We grew their sales volume dramatically.

Four years later, Fred Rogers, now the VP of sales for Broan, called to say that Nortek, the parent company of Broan/Rangaire, had purchased Nutone, and that we were fired, again.

Three months later, we received a call from Jack Stemmy, the Sales Manager of Zephyr, a new importer and distributor of range hoods, headquartered in San Francisco. They hired the former California Rangaire sales representative, who offered us the new Zephyr range hood line.

We agreed to have him fly in from San Francisco with his samples to our offices and then to see retailers together.

Our first sales call was to the biggest customer in the marketplace, P.C. Richard & Son. They had about 20 stores at the time. General Merchandise Manager Doug Kelly and buyer Jim Smith listened to our presentation. They were surprised by the quietness, power, and prices of the range hoods and proposed to be the only Zephyr dealer in the New York for one year and the assurance they would buy a lot. We agreed.

Then we added Tops Appliance in New Jersey since they were not a competitor. Soon Zephyr found another OEM manufacturer of range hoods in Fabriano, Italy to buy to also supply them. They added eight or 10 range hood models. The Fabriano manufacturer previously made range hoods for companies like GE, JennAir, and Whirlpool.

We sold to everyone including the four NY/NJ buying co-operatives with their 400-plus appliance retailers. We designed our own wood wall display.

We had the best profitability and service of any range hood brand line.

Zephyr became the leading brand in the Northeast. Eleven

years later, in 2009, Broan bought Zephyr for millions and we were fired, again.

There seemed to be a trend developing.

Craig and I contacted three manufacturers of range hoods from that same town in Fabriano, Italy. This time we were planning to have our own U.S trademark brand made for us by a well-known, high-quality manufacturer.

We chose the best one of the three. We selected one company as our source, filed for a U.S. trademark name, XO, became their exclusive importer for the U.S. and began marketing our own brand. (www.xoappliance.com).

Our preference has always been to partner with a reliable appliance manufacturer. It is ironic that we were forced into this because someone repeatedly diminished, dismissed, and rejected our efforts on their behalf and chose instead to be adversarial.

BIG COMPANIES CAN MAKE ANYTHING
THEY SELL BECOME BIG

IN 1969, I READ IN *HOME Furnishings Daily* that Sanyo Electric from Japan was coming to the U.S. I contacted them. The VP of sales for TVs, had already chosen a salesperson he had worked with previously to be his sales rep company for the New York metropolitan area. That's how that works.

He did, however, suggest that I contact the new sales manager for the Sanyo Appliance Division. I did, but I was not impressed because they had little to sell—just a few dormitory refrigerators, a portable washer, and some small appliances that were still in the works.

Introducing a manufacturer to a new market requires a lot of missionary work. Their small offering meant there would probably not be much profit initially for a great deal of effort.

I told him that I would think about it and let him know if I would take the line. I told my wife about what I had seen, and my reservations. She said, "Don't be short-sighted. Don't miss this opportunity. Big companies can become big in anything they want to sell. They have all the resources at their disposal. Grab the line or someone else will." She was smart.

She was right, again. We became the first sales rep company for Sanyo Electric's Appliance Division. In my last year with them, we sold $30,000,000 worth of their products in New York, New Jersey, Massachusetts, Connecticut, Rhode Island, New Hampshire, Vermont, and Maine.

1977: Marketing East's New England appointment for Sanyo Electric. Mort Tillman, Nubihero Arimoto, Donald Roy, Ernie Rosier, & Marty Friedman.

The Two Guys discount department stores had 200,000-sq.-ft. stores in the northeast states. Their headquarters was close by in East Hanover, New Jersey.

At that time, I was selling them the Aiwa recorders for their forty stores, but I had difficulty selling them our other brands because there were apparently special relationships their buyers had with their existing vendors, and they usually did not change suppliers.

One day, their general merchandise manager, George Lewis, mentioned in passing that he wanted to learn to play tennis and didn't know where to go for that. I told him that I was a good player, and that I would be happy to teach him the game. Most Sunday mornings, I would reserve two hours at a clay court that was located conveniently near both of our homes.

As soon as we were appointed the sales agency for Sanyo Appliance, I told him about our new product line, Sanyo. He said that Two Guys sold a lot of under-counter refrigerators and cube refrigerators for college students going back to school. I asked him if he could give me some idea of what they were paying their current supplier for the brand that they were selling.

He did that for me, but we didn't tell the buyer. The buyer told me that he was definitely not interested in making any changes. Then, because his GMM suggested to him that he at least see the new Sanyo products in person and hear what their pricing would be, he said that he would look. The buyer then allowed me to ship him two Sanyo sample refrigerators. I unpacked them in the buyer's office and the appointment was set up for my formal presentation.

The GMM was not invited to our meeting. I showed the buyer our extra features and pricing and then luckily, we got a surprise visit from the GMM, who happened to walk into the buyer's office.

When I gave the buyer my prices, which were lower, the GMM said, "How do Marty's prices compare?" He already knew that they were lower.

The buyer conceded that the Sanyo prices were good, but in this category, he said, most manufacturers cannot deliver large quantities because it is such a seasonal business, and Two Guys probably needs more than Sanyo can supply.

"How many would you need for your first order, if you would give us an opportunity?" I asked. "About 1,000 for the first order," was his reply.

I tried not to appear shocked, but I never realized that they sold so many.

I called the Sanyo headquarters in Moonachie, New Jersey and they said that they had plenty of inventory. In fact, they had recently loaded thousands of these refrigerators into their Moonachie warehouse.

Then the GMM said, "Maybe we should order the first thousand with another thousand for back-up because we both know that last year in the middle of the season, we and the supplier were both sold out and we couldn't get any more."

So, on my first day selling Sanyo appliances, I got an order for 2,000 Sanyo refrigerators. It was the first purchase order Sanyo received.

Marty Friedman and Marketing East were heroes for the Sanyo Appliance Division then and for the next 18 years. We did sales training in all the Two Guys' stores. They advertised the Sanyo refrigerators early and often and even influenced other retailers to get on board and sell Sanyo appliances.

Nothing sells like success.

We also sold them to 400 appliance retailers who were members of the five buying co-ops in the northeast.

2005 Eastern Marketing Team Photo at Crestmont.

Then Two Guys added the Sanyo portable clothes washers to compete with Panasonic, Toshiba, and others. Because we invested the time and effort to provide sales training in their stores and other competitors did not, we outsold the other brands. Eventually Two Guys stopped displaying and selling the other brands. Retail salespeople sell what they know and the company that they feel will have their back when a problem does occur.

Our business continued to grow. Two Guys expanded nationally to 97 stores.

As additional products came on the market, we introduced microwave ovens, air conditioners, big refrigerators, stacked washers and dryers. Their account provided a great boost to our overall business, and finally opened the door to other brands. Eventually, we grew to become one of their biggest suppliers. Sanyo sales in 1985 were $30 million.

Years later, Two Guys closed their retail stores, kept the properties and became the Vornado real estate company.

STICK TO THE BUSINESS YOU KNOW

IN 1973, I WAS IN BERMUDA with my wife on vacation at a luxury hotel. That year the U.S. Tennis Association refused to allow South Africa, which had an apartheid government, to participate in that year's championship, which was won by Australia's Rod Laver.

Lew Hoad, from Australia, was # 1 in the world in 1955. In 1970 he and Abe Segal, a ranked player from South Africa came to Bermuda instead of going to Wimbledon in England. My wife and I were on vacation at that same hotel. One hot afternoon, . Hoad and Segal gave a tennis doubles exhibition at the hotel.

I played tennis that afternoon with my wife on a different court.

In the locker room, Abe Segal introduced himself and asked me what I did for a living. He said he was looking for someone in sales in the U.S. who could help him and Hoad introduce their new Lew Hoad brand of tennis clothing to American retailers. He asked me if I did business with department stores. I said yes.

He said that he had a can't-miss business opportunity for me that involved sports clothing with the brand name Lew Hoad. They wanted me to be their sales agent for the U.S. and they said that I could make millions in that business. I told them that I still wasn't interested. I didn't have time because I was too busy with my own successful business. He then suggested that my wife and I have dinner that night with him and Hoad. I told him that I would introduce him to the VP of sales at Abraham & Strauss in New York and to the 100-store Zayre's, buyer in Framingham, MA.

Corrine was absolutely thrilled having dinner with Lew Hoad, the handsome blond-haired, blue-eyed Australian tennis legend.

I took Abe to Abraham & Strauss's headquarters store in Brooklyn to meet their VP of sales where he showed them his samples. Abe quoted his prices for the Lew Hoad colorful shirts, shorts, jackets, and sweaters. The merchandise was beautiful and nicely packaged.

The VP and the buyer agreed that they wanted to buy the merchandise and they asked that additional samples be sent to them. Then they would write the first purchase orders.

Wow. Then Abe Segal said to me: "Are you convinced now? Make the appointment with Zayre's and we will sell them, too."

Zayre's (now Marshalls, T.J. Maxx, Home Goods, TJC on the New York Stock Exchange) had 100-plus discount department stores in the U.S. They were headquartered in Framingham, MA. The owner and founder was Morris Feldberg.

Abe showed the samples and the prices to the VP and the buyer, who said everything was outstanding. They said that the pricing was great, but they needed a label with country of origin and the washing instructions. Abe said that was no problem. They could do that.

Then the son of the owner of the company, Mr. Feldberg, came into the room and said that he loved tennis. He heard that Lew Hoad was in the building and wanted to meet him. Lew was not with us because he had returned to his tennis camp in Malaga, Spain. Then Mr. Feldberg, asked his VP if they were going to buy this new brand for their 100 stores, and he said yes.

Then he said he had a great idea: "Once a year, all my store managers come for a Managers Sales Meeting. This year it will be at a new luxury hotel in Miami Beach. He would like Lew Hoad and Abe Segal to come as his guests and play in a tennis exhibition that all his managers would see.

Mr. Feldberg's partner would be Lew Hoad. Another Zayre's executive would be Abe Segal's partner"

Abe said yes. That was to be the following month. Everything looked great.

It was 1974. It was fun and exciting to have my wife and I with professional athletes on such a venture. We flew together back to NJ. They stayed at my home. They asked if we would like to go to the U.S. Open Tennis Championship at Forest Hills, New York with them that week? "Of course," I said. "But we don't have tickets"

Abe said, "We don't have tickets either, but we will get in." I drove, per their directions, in my Cadillac to the player's entrance. The gate attendant asked for our tickets, and we said just look in the back seat and see Lew Hoad.

"No problem," they said. "Go."

After Abe spoke to some people, we got into to the stadium without ticket. Then they moved out four people who were sitting in the best seats. That's where the four of us sat.

At the pause in the activity, we went to the food area to have a bite to eat. On the way, a celebrity ran to intercept us because he was anxious to see Lew Hoad. That was the comedian/actor/director Alan King. He immediately started to tell Lew that he was producing a Celebrity Tennis Tournament at Caesars Palace and they needed to have Lew attend.

Then Lew said "Of course you know my friends, the Friedmans." Alan King's response was "Absolutely!" Then he gave me a hug and said: "How the hell have you been. How are you?" That was amazing.

We also had an opportunity to attend private parties that night with their friends, the tennis champions Ken Rosewall and Roy Emerson.

Unfortunately, the Lew Hoad clothesline was not successful for several important reasons that anyone with experience in that industry would have known.

The decision to sell clothing made in South Africa at that time was a problem because the United States had imposed sanctions and importation bans because of the apartheid laws. You cannot lie about the country of origin.

I learned later that the pricing didn't include freight charges from South Africa or duty charges. They never hired an import agency to clear the merchandise into the USA. Abe Segal didn't understand about requiring washing instructions. The beautiful colors on the shorts, shirts, jackets, and sweaters ran when washed in a washing machine.

No wonder the numbers were so attractive. These were all costly neophyte mistakes. That whole enterprise was doomed to fail, but fortunately I hadn't committed to anything but some time. We had unbelievable experiences and I still had my successful sales agency for the TV and appliance business.

I learned the lesson of sticking to the business you know. The farther you stray from what you know, the less likely you are to succeed. In this case, I was relying on other people to cover the details. They didn't know any more than I did. They didn't do their homework. The fact that they and I weren't familiar with that business should have inspired all of us to do greater due diligence, not less.

Before Joining the Family Business, Get Experience Elsewhere

M Y SON, CRAIG, WHO HAD ATTENDED the University of Miami, always wanted to be in the business. He was always good at selling my radio samples to his teachers and anyone he could find who was interested.

After suffering a motorcycle accident when on vacation, he decided that his college education was not teaching him what he needed to learn. He said that going to the University of Miami was a waste of my money and his time. He was learning how to drink beer and to party. He said that I should put that money into a savings account for him to use as a down payment loan on his first house and let him learn the business.

He convinced me. In his sophomore year, he quit college. He said that he would be ready to go in a couple of weeks.

Craig was shocked when I told him that we don't hire inexperienced salespeople. He would have to acquire experience somewhere else. He then applied for a job in the electronics department at the Bloomingdale's store in Short Hills. He told the H.R. woman that all of the employees in their electronics department were too old and unfamiliar with the new electronics products that young people were looking to buy. He was right.

She said that she was impressed with him, but they had no immediate sales positions open. Perhaps if he would start with a position in their warehouse and when a position would open up, she would transfer him. Craig surprised her by saying he didn't have time to waste doing that, but he would be interested should the job selling become available. Then he left.

He returned a week later to see if he could change the person's mind to hire him. He reminded her that they were losing sales having only older salespeople in that electronics department.

They hired him. He became the top retail salesperson in the electronics department at that store. In fact, the buyer, who I dealt with in NYC, told me that Craig had increased volume so much that his Short Hills store moved from #8 to #2 in sales. Only the flagship Manhattan store had outsold them.

After four years with Bloomingdale's, Craig joined Marketing East Industries Corp., first detailing stores, and then selling the most difficult Manhattan customers, like a retailer from India, Danny Dandona, an Orthodox Jewish retailer, David Friedman, Korean retailers, and Chinese retailers.

After a number of successful years, he wanted to sell some giant retailers, but previously I had taken on two junior partners and they objected. My recommendation was that we each agree to give one big account to Craig, but they would not agree.

So, on my recommendation, Craig left my employ and joined another sales company as their NJ representative. They sold BASF audio and videocassettes, electronic games, TVs from Taiwan, and electronics throughout the New York area. His territory was New Jersey, and he did very well selling all the big accounts, like Trader Horn, as well as the smaller accounts.

I continued to grow Marketing East.

Once a year, we attended the largest national show for electronics called the Consumer Electronics Show (CES) in Chicago. This was where manufacturers showed off their newest merchandise.

All the retail buyers, including the biggest, attended the show and had to wait in line for their food. As with most tradeshows, attendees ate lunch at food stands, enduring long lines and high prices. In 1977, I decided to show our appreciation for the dealers. I sponsored a private luncheon during the first day of the show in one of the building's largest dining rooms, the Dr. Lawless Room. We paid top dollar and demanded the best food for our buffet lunch, but it was money well invested.

Our private luncheon allowed invited guests to see the biggest accounts. It made me feel special. It was lucky that we made it by invitation only and that we had guards at the door to see their invitations, because we had to turn away many retailers who were not on our invited guest list.

We did a similar private luncheon the next year at the CES Show in Las Vegas. Our competitors never followed our lead.

It makes you feel good to give back. This was giving back. In our placards at the entrance, we called it: "The Marketing East Dealer Appreciation Luncheon."

EBA Appl. Tony Tesoriero, Key Appl. Brooklyn, Co-Op with Eastern Marketing's Joe Cacciatore, Craig & Marty Friedman.

I Lose My Company

IN 1985, THE PRICE OF OIL plunged to only $24. a barrel, causing the producers to reduce availability. That caused a shortage of fuel for home heating and for driving cars. As a substitute for heating homes that winter, manufacturers began selling kerosene heaters in the USA. They were sold by Panasonic, Sharp, Sears, Sanyo, and others.

We sold them to all the regional Home Centers in NY, NJ and New England, including Channel Lumber, Rickels, Somerville Lumber, and all our 400 appliance retailers who took a chance trying something new with us. We did millions that year with Sanyo kerosene heaters.

In 1986, we were shocked to hear from our Sanyo VP that Sanyo would not be selling Sanyo Kerosene Heaters. That would mean a loss of about $150,000 in commission for Marketing East.

Unknown to all of the six Sanyo sales agency companies was that someone had purchased all the Sanyo kerosene heaters, apparently under a fictitious name.

These thousands of cartons were stored in my friend's public warehouse instead of the Sanyo warehouse in Bergen County,

NJ. My friend, who owned that warehouse told me that someone (not Sanyo) rented space in his warehouse in Edison, NJ and he showed me the three Sanyo spec sheets for the models that he was storing there.

I met with the VP who told me not to tell anyone about this, or I would be fire—even though I had a contract for commission for all Sanyo products sold.

The next day, I told my two junior partners, and the following day one of them met with the Sanyo VP.

The following day, my two junior partners invited me to an emergency meeting where they notified me that our company bank account and the locks to our office were changed. They sent a letter to all our customers that "Marty Friedman has retired." They told me that I was officially out of my company.

After consulting with four different attorneys about my rights, they all advised me to sue the people who took over my company. I called the Sanyo VP and was told that sometimes that the way it works.

I then decided to sue and start my new sales agency company immediately. We had been the biggest sales agency, with $30,000,000 in sales. We were doing 40 percent of the Sanyo appliance business in the USA.

It was my time start all over time again at age 57.

That week, I contacted all our manufacturers and all of the appliance makers. They terminated their relationships with my old company and hired me and my new company. They all said that they didn't understand how I could be terminated from the company that I owned and founded and was in charge of.

The brands that terminated my Marketing East company and hired me were Premier ranges, Rangaire range hoods, Welbilt refrigerators, General freezers, refrigerators, and dehumidifiers.

The brands that stayed with Marketing East were: Sanyo appliances, Southwestern Bell Telephone, Freedom Phone, Uniden radar detectors, and Bearcat scanners.

Nationwide CT Buying Coop Presentation, Hartford, CT.

I couldn't afford to pay the salespeople and therefore I had to rebuild my new company, doing the selling myself. Corrine stepped in again as my office manager and customer service point person.

Two years after I was removed from the sales company that I founded; the two junior partners settled my lawsuit. I collected money.

All the retailers in the USA who bought the Sanyo kerosene heaters the previous two years from Sanyo were later notified by Sanyo to place their purchase orders for the same products from the fictitious company with payables to that company with a P.O. Box address in Boston, MA.

I believe that I was removed from my own company, Marketing East, because I was a threat to reveal and disrupt a plan to sell all the kerosene heaters that year through the fictitious distributor. Someone could make millions of dollars and we would not receive any commissions.

Once more, I worked seven days and six nights a week to build a business. Craig said that he would join the new company and help grow it as soon as I could afford to pay him.

Marketing East, went out of business a few years after the court settlement. Sanyo left the USA appliance business a few years after that because they said that business was not good enough to stay in the USA.

Recently the Sanyo Appliance Division was sold to the world's largest manufacturer of appliances, Haier of China.

Forty years later I had a drink with one of my former partners, who told me the rest of the story about my departure as he knew it. At that time, he was in bad health, broke, and asked me for a loan or gift of money. I said no. The Sanyo VP died from cancer 5 years later. I believe she was in her sixties.

BE TRUE TO YOUR BELIEFS
AND PRINCIPLES OF FAIRNESS

IN 1983, THE WELBILT BRAND WAS dominant in the low-end, apartment house gas-range business. The company was owned by Raytheon Corporation, the giant defense contractor who is the leading supplier of guided missiles to the United States. Their old, high-volume, low-cost gas range manufacturing facility was in rural Pennsylvania.

Most of my dealers complained that their Welbilt representative was nasty and disinterested in their business. He always packed imitation Rolex watches, made in China, that he was anxious to sell for $25.00.

Every retailer bought the Welbilt gas ranges because their prices were so much lower than the other brands. They were the standard for rental apartments and for subsidized low-income housing, where the tenant takes whatever they can get.

Many of the retailers that we were calling on said that if they had a brand that was somewhat competitive, they would love to switch their business away from Welbilt.

Based on their input, I was sure that there was an opportunity if I could find the right manufacturer of gas ranges. I traveled to

Tennessee to see the White Westinghouse company, who offered me their Vesta brand of gas ranges. We sold their products for about six months but their marketing was all wrong, and they were not interested in changing.

In March 1986, we became the sales agency for the Peerless Premier Appliance Company of Belleville, Illinois. Premier was founded in 1912. They originally manufactured cast iron and wood and coal stoves, and operated one of the few facilities to manufacture porcelain. Then and now, porcelain is the coating used for gas range parts. They made gas ranges and electric ranges in sizes 20", 24", 30", and 36" widths.

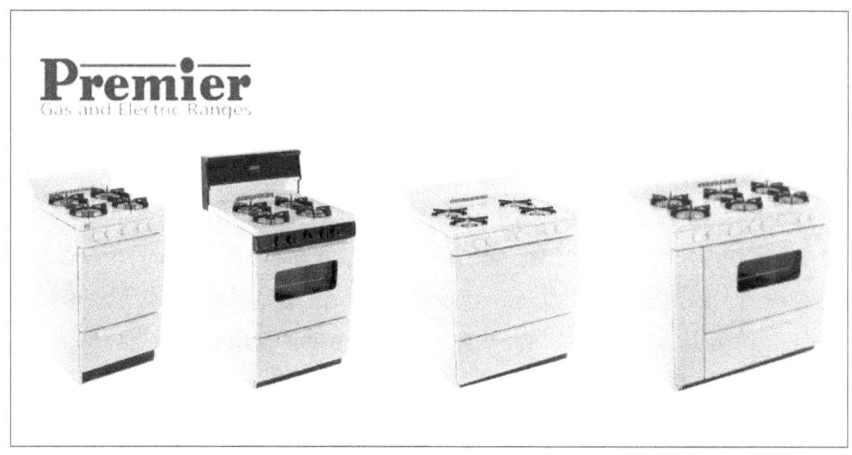

1986: Premier Ranges.

The merchandise manager for Key Appliance Co-op of Brooklyn [50 appliance retail co-op owners], told me that if the factory could reduce prices to be more competitive, then he would be happy to be our first customer. In order to reduce prices, he recommended taking out a few quality features that Welbilt didn't have. I called the Premier sales manager and told him about the customer's suggestion. I asked if they could possibly take out the big broiler, for example, since Welbilt only used a single pipe for a broiler even though it can't broiler or bake evenly.

The sales manager told me that they didn't manufacture cheap products and that they only wanted to make and sell products that they could be proud of.

I then asked him how many ranges are needed to get the freight to be paid by Premier. It is 950 miles away from Belleville, IL to Brooklyn. He said, "Orders of 24 ranges or more is delivered freight prepaid." Then I asked: "How many ranges are in a truckload? Would it cost the factory less for freight if my customer bought in truckloads only?"

His answer was "NOBODY BUYS A TRUCKLOAD." That's when I said the freight has to be a major factor especially for trucking charges to travel 950 miles. "HOW MANY RANGES WILL FIT IN A FULL TRUCKLOAD, and how much would the prices be if someone ordered a full truckload?"

He called me back and told me that 98 of the 24" ranges, and 100 to 120 with a mixed load of 20", 24", 30", and 36" ranges. Then an hour later he called to tell me that he was surprised to learn that there is a savings of $15 less for the Premier basic models and $20 to $25 for the Premier deluxe models. That's all we needed!

Now the new Premier prices were much closer in price to the lesser quality Welbilt ranges. In addition to the significant savings that truckload pricing provided, there would be less damages because small shipments usually are unloaded and re-loaded at different warehouse locations. Key Appliance Co-op wrote the first truckload order for the Premier ranges for delivery to their warehouse in Brooklyn, NY.

I had found an opportunity that was good for the manufacturer and for the dealers. This was exactly the start that we needed in order to make this a big business for us and our new manufacturer of gas and electric ranges, who previously sold very little in the east.

I told that first truckload customer that he had his choice as to the brand name because Peerless Premier had taken oven the brand names for the gas range manufacturers that they originally provided the porcelain coating for, and therefore they had different trade names for their ranges, if needed.

They could make them as Premier, Eagle, Modern Chef, Mark Royal, and Heritage. He said he didn't care what name was on the product, so I assigned Mark Royal, a brand that had never been sold in New York before. Frankly, I thought that was not the strongest brand name, but he liked it.

Next, I held a dealer show at a hotel in Long Island that was close to the headquarters of the largest retailer, P.C. Richard & Son. I invited Billy Traywick, the merchandise manager of the 20-store retailer to be the first one to see the merchandise.

He said that he would be there at 10 a.m. The merchandise manager of the second largest Long Island retailer, Newmark & Lewis, had his appointment at 11 a.m. The P.C. buyer didn't show up for his appointment, and when I called him, he said that he was too busy that day and he would try to make it tomorrow.

The merchandise manager from Newmark & Lewis arrived on time. We reviewed the prices and the features. Then he asked if P.C. Richard had seen this merchandise and the program. I said: "Not yet." He said, "If I can have this line without them having the line, tell him not to come." He said that I should come to his office and he would give me my first order for my first truckload of the exclusive Eagle ranges for New York.

I told him that I planned to sell the Eagle brand to Tops Appliance and their stores in NJ, which he said was fine. I told him that Key Appliance had already ordered the Modern Chef brand ranges. He said that he had no problem with different brands for different retailers. In fact, he said, that gives everyone a better opportunity to make more money.

Every "Yes" was another truckload order.

My salespeople and I taught the salespeople in the stores the features and benefits of our products. That helped. It meant more early days and late evenings out, and I loved it. I was once more "a traveling preacher" helping retailers to increase their profits and sell features and benefits. I was doing what made me first fall in love with the business, helping people and being appreciated.

I sold the Eagle brand in New York to Newmark & Lewis, and to Tops Appliance in New Jersey. I sold Premier brand to Appliance Dealers Coop in NJ and later to the Intercounty Appliance Co-Op in Long Island. I sold the Modern Chef brand to a builder-distributor in New York.

When I saw the Welbilt salesman in the reception area at Newmark & Lewis shortly after they received their first Eagle shipment, he informed me that if I thought that Peerless Premier would be able to compete with him, then I was sadly mistaken. He said Raytheon is the owner of Welbilt. They have loads of money, and Premier is a nobody. He said that they could put us out of business any time they desired by simply lowering prices for a few months. Premier didn't have the finances to be able to compete with a manufacturer who was willing to lose money to eliminate a competitor. That is how Rockefeller, and J.P. Morgan built their businesses, forcing others out of business.

He had already recommended that they do just that, and that we would soon be out of business in New York. "Don't be surprised when it happens. Your gas range line will be finished in this territory," he told me smugly.

The Peerless Premier gas range business continued to grow in New York and New Jersey and we even expanded with Key Appliance Co-op in Connecticut (40 stores) and Nationwide of Connecticut Co-Op and their 50 stores in Hartford.

I did have a problem trying to sell the Premier brand to Intercounty Appliance Co-op (65 stores) in New York because the buyer was very friendly with the Welbilt salesman and would not even hear our program or pricing or features. I made an appointment with the president of Intercounty and told him. He arranged for me to show my Premier ranges and make a presentation at the next Dealer Meeting at a hotel in Long Island.

After the presentation the dealers were allowed to ask questions and place orders. Then the buyer told me to come to his office the next week and he would give me the truckload order of Premier ranges for New York.

That morning, the buyer told me that "he lost his dealer's orders" but he would still give me an order. He continued to make it difficult for me. Six months later, when their president heard what he was continuing to do to me, they fired him.

After I had sold all five buying co-ops, it was time to see the biggest customer of ranges in New York—The New York City Housing Authority.

Welbilt was the only supplier of gas ranges to this account. They supplied ranges for the 40,000 low-income, government-subsidized NYC apartments.

I registered, and went to the next public bid for 350 gas ranges at the NYC municipal building to watch and learn.

Welbilt was the lowest bidder. Hotpoint, Westinghouse, Whirlpool, Premier, and others bid, but Welbilt won the bid. I then made an appointment to meet the buyer to discuss why they should be using our ranges. He explained that the people who get these ranges and refrigerators are people with little or no money, who are living in subsidized housing, and they are happy to get anything free with which they can cook. He said the NYCHA is only interested in saving money by supplying the refrigerators and gas ranges to every subsidized apartment with the lowest costs.

Instead of giving up, I went to a housing project where they were delivering their next shipment of Welbilt ranges. The superintendent said that they have been receiving only Welbilt ranges for as long as he had been there. He said they have all the parts needed for the Welbilt because they buy them from Welbilt every month and also do all their own service free for Welbilt.

He didn't know that the Welbilt's pricing included FREE SERVICE & PARTS FOR ONE YEAR, and that any dealer choosing to do their own service gets the parts free and is paid $150. or more for every Welbilt range they service.

Then I returned to the biggest gas range purchaser in New York City, the New York City Housing Authority and I told the buyer that every other Welbilt retailer gets free parts and free service for one year. Unless they are giving him extra money for not receiving service and parts, then he has been overpaying Welbilt all those years.

I also told him that the maintenance costs with our Premier brand were much lower because the Premier brand ranges didn't break down as often. To prove my point, I suggested that he call the biggest service agency that does in-warranty service for Welbilt and Premier and speak to the owner. I gave him the name and direct phone number of that service agency. I said that he should just ask him about the quality of each brand.

He was concerned to hear what I told him and said that he would verify what I had told him.

The next bid for gas ranges, was a small bid and we were again higher priced than Welbilt, but the buyer awarded the order to us for the Premier ranges.

When I saw the buyer the next week to ask him why we received the bid when we didn't have the lowest price, he said that they always have the right to try another brand if they chose.

The next few bids had the same result.

Then a bid was announced for 1,000 ranges. At the bid, I heard them announce the Welbilt bid, and it was about 20 percent lower than our Premier bid.

After the bids were announced, I telephoned the Premier sales manager to tell him that Welbilt won the bid and told him their pricing.

He said: "Marty, they didn't win. They just chose to lose money."

He was right. Two days later I heard that an executive from Welbilt called the NYHA buyer to say that they could not honor the quote and asked if they could get out of the contract. They were told that they had to fulfill the contract or they would be sued. That executive got fired.

Apparently, what had happened was that someone at Raytheon learned of the bid and the amount of the loss that they were going to have, and fired the person responsible. Then they reviewed the Welbilt profitability and decided to sell the company!

They didn't find a buyer after six months and decided to sell off the manufacturing equipment in Pennsylvania at a public auction. All the parts to manufacture the ranges were sold to different companies.

The Welbilt company went out of the gas and electric range business including their very popular brands of Sunray, Glenwood and Welbilt.

NYC Housing Authority then switched all their manual clean gas ranges to Premier. Even today the New York City Housing Authority every year buys only the Premier gas ranges.

It seems that financially sound giant corporations may be in a position to lose money, but they don't like to own businesses that are not profitable.

I take no enjoyment in the demise of a competitor. But this was a growing experience. I can look back on this episode and say that I was right.

I played it fair and square, and we won.

When we started with the line, I learned that the Premier truckload shipments often had five or 10 ranges that were being damaged with each shipment. I attended a 7:00 a.m. delivery to a New York warehouse.

When the driver opened the doors of the trailer, I saw that the last two rows of the 100-plus ranges were upside down and laying sideways. They had not been secured at all.

I asked the driver, who could see the units that apparently were damaged, why that happened and how that could be corrected.

He said that traveling 1,000 miles over bumpy roads without using restraining bars on the last row of ranges causes the problem.

I asked how we could get the restraining bars. His reply was that every tractor trailer keeps them for every delivery, but they don't install them unless it is requested by the shipper. He continued that if you want the delivery to be even more secure, you can request air bags to be installed to fill in the rear, in addition to the restraining bar, but that costs additional money.

After that, every Premier range shipment had restraining bars to reduce freight damage. I love to learn.

DIFFERENT GOALS FOR DIFFERENT FOLKS

IN 1987 SALES WERE GETTING EVEN better, and I was looking for additional salespeople for my fairly new Eastern Marketing Corp.

At Mr. Jay's Appliance on Long Island, I saw a really good retail salesman who I thought would be a good addition to my company. He was Joe Cacciatore from Chicago. Joe told me that he expected to find a position soon as a wholesale salesperson with Whirlpool. I told him that we would love to hire him, but we don't hire talent from our retailer customers.

Months later, I learned that he had left his retail sales position and was now working for the Amana distributor in New York. I asked Joe if he would be interested in joining my company. He said that he doubted that we could pay him as much as he was already making. When I asked him if he would consider joining our team if we could offer that same amount, he said that he still wasn't interested. He said he was going to stay where he was because it was easier to sell the popular branded products.

Joe was a hard worker and I was sure that he would do well selling our brands, so I tried to figure out what I could offer him to make a change.

He was this big ego guy and big physically. He was driving a small leased economy car which is what distributors normally provided. The next time I saw him; I commented that I had heard that he was doing well as a top salesman for Amana.

I said, "Why are you still squeezing into an economy vehicle instead of driving a successful man's car? A luxury car shows success for a successful guy like you."

His answer was: "So if I was with Eastern Marketing, I could be driving a Cadillac?"

"Maybe."

Then we left the issue for further discussion.

The next Sunday morning, I called Joe and asked if he would like to meet me at Potamkin Cadillac on 12th Avenue in NYC. He didn't ask why, but he agreed to meet me there at 12 noon.

Joe and I and a Cadillac salesman went to the second floor where all their new cars were parked. Joe looked and looked until he found a brand-new Cadillac Eldorado that he liked.

"Sit in it," I said He sat in the driver's seat and looked like he had fallen in love.

"This would be really for me if I join your team?"

I said, "Yes, it's your decision." Then he happily agreed to join our team.

Joe did a great job in the three years that he was with us. But when the lease ran out on the car, he left us to go to Whirlpool, first as a sales manager, then as their KitchenAid division Sales Manager.

Hire the best you can. That's my philosophy.

Manufactures Know How to Make Good Products, but They May Not Know How to Sell Their Products

IN 1988, WE WERE CONTACTED BY Marvel Refrigeration in Richmond, Indiana, to be their sales agency for their forced-air, under-counter built-in refrigerators.

Their previous distributor, W.R. Light, had filed Chapter 7 bankruptcy, because they lost their biggest line of appliances, and could not find a replacement.

We were recommended and offered the line to sell as Marvel's sales representatives.

I went to the factory to learn about their business. It was located in a very poor town, next to farm country in western Ohio. They made their built-in, under-counter refrigerators there. Most retailers sold the U-Line brand, which was manufactured in Milwaukee. All of the most successful distributors were selling their products.

Before visiting the Marvel facility, I understood that the costs for Marvel were $20 and $30 higher than the popular U-Line brand. Jim Coye, the Marvel General manager could not explain why they were priced higher than their major competitor. The Marvel dealers did not know the reason either.

I went to the factory, spoke to the management there, and

received a tour of the facility. Then I looked by myself and found an engineering department and a research department. I saw engineers in white medical coats doing experiments with various refrigerators. When I looked in their warehouse, I saw that most of the inventory for delivery was with cartons labeled Cardinal Healthcare [largest hospital supply distributor], Fischer Scientific, and Marvel Scientific. There were not many Marvel cartons being staged for shipment.

When I asked the engineers what the difference was between their hospital and scientific refrigerators and the Marvel brand, they said that there was no difference. Only the brand name plate on the front and the electric plug are different. They were exactly the same because it would cost too much to have two different production lines.

I learned that the Marvel compressor, was 40 percent more powerful [467 btus-cubic feet per minute air flow] vs the U-Line brand at 280 btus. That meant that the Marvel units could hold the set point temperature [exact temperature] and the U-Line models could not. The Marvel would turn on and off less often. Marvel would last longer and require less service because it was a commercial refrigerator being sold as a residential refrigerator.

The Marvel fan blower, which cooled off the compressor to prevent over-heating was metal with five large fan blades vs the U-Line that had four small plastic fan blades with a plastic base.

Based on what I learned at the factory, it was understandable the Marvel models should cost the consumer $50 more because they were commercial units being sold for the residential market. What we needed to do was to explain the advantages, and the better value to dealers, their retail salespeople, and consumers.

Designers had introduced the lifestyle refrigeration category for consumers to have the convenience of refrigeration and ice in their great room, living room, den, bar, etc. The refrigerator would fit under the countertop.

Such a refrigerator needed a powerful compressor to keep the temperature constant, and a fan blower at the bottom of the unit to cool the compressor so it would not overheat. U-Line was the first manufacturer to understand the need.

Since the retailers, retail salespeople, and consumers didn't know anything about this, it was our job to teach them in order to be successful.

When I went to the stores, I found there was a yellow warning sign on the front glass door of every U-Line. It was a warning to vacuum out the bottom vent three or four times a year. Failure to clean out the dust would block the air flow. The heat would ruin the compressor. The consumer who spends $1,500 or $2,000 for their built-in undercounter refrigerator for their den or great room, with expensive wood cabinetry, probably spends $20,000 or $30,000, and never does the vacuuming themselves. That's the job of the housecleaner. If the consumer knew that the Marvel was better, many would be willing to pay more.

One of the first things we found was that the model numbers that Marvel were using were warehouse parts numbers that did not explain what was in the box. That was typical thinking for a manufacturer who didn't do residential business because it simplified their record-keeping. But in the appliance business everyone uses model numbers to help understand what is inside the carton.

When Marvel wouldn't accept our advice, we created our own easy-to-understand model numbers, like a 61RF-G-B-, instead of 54LP2748 which has nothing to do with describing the item. We were trying to indicate 6.1 cu.ft. capacity. R-refrigerator F-freezer. G-glass front door. B-black cabinet. L-lock for the door.

Then for our people and the retail salespeople, we created a price booklet with the recommended retail prices and our new model numbers, with a picture of each model and the features and benefits of each model.

We asked the general manager to put our "simplified" model labels on the carton. He said they could not do that; it was "a waste of time." Finally, we agreed to pay $10 a carton and provided our own labels for the cartons. They agreed to glue our labels to the cartons that were coming to us.

A year later, the company changed their model numbering system to our model numbering system. We taught them the right way to sell appliance retailers.

We were fortunate that the undercounter refrigeration category became a "must have" because interior designers were recommending them to their clients. A few years later, U-Line announced their new wine storage unit, THE WINE CAPTAIN. They recommended it for their long-term storage that could store red and white wines at the right temperatures and the humidity. Why didn't they call it a Wine Cellar or Wine Storage like the $10,000 Wine Cellars?

1964: Sanyo undercounter refrigerator.

We figured out that their name Wine Captain was because their units were not true wine cellars. They could not maintain exact SET POINT TEMPERATURE because of their inferior 280 btu compressor and plastic four-blade cooling fans. They would probably get sued if they called their units wine cellars.

Marvel, with their commercial refrigerators, could be called wine cellars and maintain exact temperatures, along with the correct humidity, but instead, all the marvel literature said, "Marvel Wine Coolers"; not "Marvel Wine Cellars." Another mistake. If they had taken my advice and called their units wine cellars, instead of wine coolers, they would have increased their sales by 20 percent because they were commercial units that were actually wine cellars. They didn't ask us or listen to us because they always thought they knew best.

In January 1991, Iraq invaded Kuwait. The response by the U.S. was called "Operation Desert Storm." Marvel made 13,000 medical commercial refrigerators for the U.S. Army field hospitals. They were commercial units; not like the U-Line products.

Gordon Stauffer, the owner of Marvel, had contacted the U.S. government and arranged for the sale. They were all made in green for the U.S. army and one was on display at the factory.

A few years later, Gordon Stauffer, then chairman of AHAM [American Home Appliance Manufacturers] arranged to build the built-in, undercounter refrigerators, and wine cellars for the General Electric Company, and for the Viking Corp because the category was important for the Kitchen Appliance business. That increased the volume for buying more parts at a time and lowered their parts costs. The two OEM customers did help influence improvements in the Marvel products.

In 1991, U-Line invented a system of wood-framed, front-glass-door models that allowed the kitchen cabinets to match their under-counter refrigeration and Wine Captains.

Our sales for NY, NJ, New England, were excellent. At our national sales meeting in Richmond, IN, I asked the Marvel sales manager when we could expect the wood framed units so we could compete.

He said: "We are working on it."

A year later, Sub-Zero was selling wood-framed glass-door models. Because I had been told that 30 percent of that business was now the matching glass door models with wood framing, I asked again at the sales meeting with Marvel. The sales manager said, "Marty, you have to be a little more patient, our engineering department is still working on it."

One week later, while speaking on the phone with Gordon Stauffer, the Marvel owner on the phone, I asked him about making the glass doors with a darker color on our Marvel front doors. He said, "Marty, I don't know the answer because we don't even make our front doors. We use a specialty company to provide them to us."

BINGO.

I then asked for the contractor's name, and where they were located. He told me that they were in Elizabeth, New Jersey, eight miles from our office. I immediately called them and was at that facility the next morning.

The owner gave me a tour. I asked if he thought that he could make the matching wood frame glass doors for our Marvel units. He said, "Of course we can. I made them for Sub-Zero until they decided to make them for themselves." He said that Marvel never asked him to make them. I told him to make up a sample and if Marvel doesn't buy them, we will.

I immediately called the Marvel general manager and asked him to please do me a favor and check just one more time to see if they could make those wood-framed glass units for our wine cellars and refrigerators.

He did. He called back that same day to tell me that now we could make hem. We finally got our wood-framed glass doors.

At the next national sales meeting, Gordon Stauffer showed everyone the new models and thanked us for pushing to get this done.

He said they should be called, "THE MARTY FRIEDMAN DOOR." All the other Marvel Sales Reps stood up and applauded me for my efforts. That felt good.

We were never afraid to invest our own time and money to get things done. Then we finally were able to convince Marvel to appoint us as distributors for Marvel Refrigeration and their sister company Northland Refrigeration in Greenville, Michigan. That meant that we could carry inventory and not have to wait for them to ship the products. Now we were their distributors and not their sales agents. That was 1991.

Having consistent local stock of Marvel units made another major difference because having immediate local availability is important. Months later, one of our biggest customers told me: "When I get the designer's order for their appliances and for the U-Line units, I tell them to switch to Marvel because I know that Eastern Marketing will always have them in stock. The U-Line/SubZero distributor, Carl Schaedel, is frequently out of stock and it's a horror show for us because if one unit can't be delivered, then everything waits and that's a big problem."

We designed and had built for us Marvel custom wood displays to help sales.

We created our own point-of-purchase materials with signs and banners to educate the consumer and the retail salespeople about the advantages of Marvel's features and benefits.

The difference was that we checked for ourselves and understood that this small manufacturer was in business selling bio-medical and laboratory application refrigerators. They were accommodating consumers willing to pay more for their products. We helped dramatically grow their residential business and had a great relationship during our 24 years with them. We were selling more Marvel units than U-Line with their brand.

The fact that the Expo Design stores, a luxury division of Home Depot, chose to display and sell the Marvel under-counter refrigerators and wine cellars was a major boost to our sales.

Then the Great Indoors, followed with the Sears version of the luxury appliance division and we did major business with them, too.

In 2016, we were terminated two years after Marvel was purchased by Middleby Corp, a billion-dollar distributor of commercial cooking appliances—Blodget, Bakers Pride, Garland, and Turbo Chef.

Some would say that the millions of dollars that Marvel refrigeration and Northland Marvel sold for, was greatly influenced by the efforts of all those people at Eastern Marketing. It was a good run for more than two decades.

Middleby also purchased Lynx, U-Line, Viking, AGA, and La Cornue. We knew how to build manufacturers' brands. Getting fired because another entity bought them, spurred us to get a US trademarked brand of our own: XO Appliance.

We interviewed OEM [original equipment manufacturers] until we found a manufacturer who was experienced with worldwide sales had and a great reputation for reliability and quality. They manufacture the best quality and features if you are willing to pay for it. We have the know-how to sell products. They have the know-how to manufacturer the built-in undercounter refrigeration category. Our XO [xoappliance.com] brand has with all the right features and is priced 25 percent lower than the Marvel models only because they are made in China.

The following is a quote about us from, the owner of Marvel refrigeration and Northland refrigeration, Gordon Stauffer: Founding President and CEO, Marvel Industries, Richmond, IN; Founding President and CEO, Northland Marvel, Greenville, MI; Former President of Fedders Refrigeration Company. Two-time Chairman and longest standing board member of the American Home Appliance Manufacturers:

"Over my 40 years in the home appliance industry, I have leaned on our major distributors, dealers, and retailers for advice on new products and on new marketing strategies. Marty was often the only one on the other side of the equation. He and Craig have been critical to the success of both our products and our marketing programs. Read this book for the lessons it teaches about being successful in both business and life. Marty has led an amazing life and has left his indelible mark on this industry."

One of my favorite sayings is: "You don't want to be the best at what you do. You want to be the only one who does what you do."

Always Look for the Distribution Company with the Knowledge and Reputation to Best Establish Your Brand in the USA

IN 1986, WE AGREED TO DISTRIBUTE Sterling cooking appliances for New World Domestic Appliance Co., the largest manufacturer of gas ranges in the UK. For many years they were the only manufacturer of gas "cooker" ranges in the UK because they sold to only one company—British Utility, called British Gas.

We did well in New York selling their 24" cookers, cooktops, and wall ovens, with dealers like Gringer & Son, in Manhattan. But after a few years, they stopped selling in the U.S. because they could not find other distributors in the rest of the country who were looking to sell the brand,.

In 1987, we agreed to distribute Regency, a manufacturer of cooking appliances from New Zealand. We did well, but not well enough for a major manufacturer to continue in the U.S. without other volume distribution.

Manufacturers see opportunities for growth and are always looking for shortcuts to come into the United States. These are all opportunities for sales companies who know how to create businesses. It's all opportunity and fun.

The loss of these lines was never considered disappointments but rather as opportunities to seek out new lines to distribute.

Inventing a New Category:
The Outdoor Kitchen

A MANUFACTURER, WHO HEARD ABOUT OUR REPUTATION for building brands, contacted us about selling his luxury outdoor gas grill line. The brand was called ProFire, headquartered in Florida.

We investigated and found that most appliance retailers in the warm weather areas, where people can cook outdoors most months of the year, sell outdoor gas grills, sometimes called BBQs. ProFire taught us what we needed to know. Many of our appliance retailers bought and sold the merchandise, even though it was not a brand that their customers had heard of.

Later, when another competitor, DCS, realized their local distributor was also selling the Lynx brand, he gave them a choice of selling only one brand, DCS or Lynx. That distributor chose to sell only DCS. We were recommended by the dealers and became the Lynx gas grill distributors in 1996. They were the third best-selling brand at that time.

We traveled to California to see the factory and learn all that we could about the brand. Afterward we resigned from selling the other brand.

The biggest volume in the outdoor gas grill business was with units selling in a range of $500 to $1000, but there was a growing luxury market if they could be displayed where retail salespeople could explain the features and benefits that make an outdoor kitchen selling for $3,000 to $30,000 an investment in your house and provide more enjoyment in cooking.

The lower-end grills are made from cast iron and or cheaper metals and they always rust out after five years because they are not made of 304 stainless steel that resists rust. They rust even faster if they are close to oceans or lakes. Very few of our appliance retailers in the northeast sold luxury grills before we got involved. The majority of the high-priced grills were being sold by hearth dealers, grill specialists, and fireplace dealers and being built into custom islands.

If the consumer is purchasing a new home for $700,000 or more, his new indoor kitchen with appliances will usually cost $50,000. Then that consumer could afford $3,000 to $30,000 for an outdoor kitchen which can be added to the new mortgage and be an added value when the property is eventually sold.

We set up displays for many appliance retailers in the northeast. We taught the dealers how to display and sell the category. We did well.

We dramatically increased the number of appliance retailers selling Lynx luxury grills and grew the company's sales. We taught our 500 dealers how to sell more than just grills; we sold "Outdoor Kitchens," which included side burners, doors, drawers, towel dispensers, garbage shoots, ice makers, refrigerators, beer tap units, and lobster pot burners. Consumers were willing to spend the extra money on a higher-powered, faster-cooking, stainless steel, free-standing grill in an outdoor island that would last a lifetime and could grill steaks with a searing burner to cook like the steakhouses cook. That was once they knew they had an option.

We invested in this new category, showing dealers how to

promote effectively with outdoor island displays, signs, advertising materials, training, grilling events outside their stores, which we supplied. Craig even created a new category of product which we called THE OUTDOOR KITCHEN. Since the sales of outdoor kitchens is 20 percent of the volume of indoor kitchens, then the retailer should be able to figure out what his sales volume should be in that category since he usually knows his volume with his Indoor Kitchen Sales.

The third year with the line, we offered a dealer trip to Laguna Beach/Dana Point, California at a luxury hotel to see the next year's new Lynx line of Outdoor Kitchen Appliances and to play golf.

The event was super successful. We continued to learn and grow the business. Eventually we made Lynx the # 1 brand of gas grills in the USA.

In 1992, Home Depot decided to venture into high-end stores. They called them Expo Design stores. They asked SubZero, Thermador, and Viking if they could buy their merchandise for the first 10 Expo Design stores located in the Northeast.

Mickey and Mary Reali, Orville's Appliance stores, arriving from the Buffalo Airport to Eastern Marketing to see the showroom.

All three manufacturers told them that they would not allow that. These manufacturers believed that it would not be good for their image to sell retailers who had a reputation (they thought) of selling low-end products.

Since at that time, they could not buy Sub Zero or Viking undercounter refrigeration products, they were willing to try the Marvel undercounter refrigerators, wine cellars, and ice makers in all their 10 Expo Design stores. We took advantage of the opportunity and did our usually diligent efforts to teach their salespeople the features and benefits of our Marvel models.

John D. Marcella & Lori Juliani, Schenectady, NY
with Marty & Dino at the Saratoga Racetrack.

The results were excellent and our relationships with their salespeople were great. I frequently visited their headquarters in Atlanta, and that relationship grew, probably because the results in the stores was better than their other suppliers.

There were U-Line products on display in every store, but they didn't sell. When they doubled their stores nationally, we convinced management to try our Lynx grills and islands, Zephyr range hoods, and the Bertazzoni cooking line to their stores nationally.

They helped us create brand recognition for all of our brands because the traffic in their stores was unbelievable and their displays were state of the art. They were a major factor in our growth to be # 1 with Lynx.

Yet, six years later, Home Depot decided to close all their Expo Design Centers.

Yesterday, Today, and Tomorrow
IN CONSUMER SALES

SMALL, INDEPENDENT RETAILERS IN THE APPLIANCE business have always had to compete with the giants. When I first entered the business in 1956, everyone was certain that the big retailers would eliminate the "little guys." It didn't happen. Some didn't make sufficient profit, some left the retail appliance and TV business, and some went to other businesses.

Fortunately for us, around 1965, seven Brooklyn food stores formed the Key Food Buying Cooperative to compete with the giant food chains such as A&P. They bought their meat, vegetables, fruit, seafood, canned goods, etc. together to be able to charge competitive prices. Each of the original owners contributed a significant amount of money to fund the company a warehouse and employees. Each owner was responsible for buying for a different category. They were very successful.

In the late 1960s, one of th same originators of Key Food formed the appliance buying cooperative Key Appliance of Brooklyn, comprised of half a dozen TV and appliance retailers. They were very successful.

Then within 10 years, most of the TV/appliance retailers in NY/

NJ became members of one of the five buying cooperatives. They purchased 85 percent of their merchandise from their groups. This allowed them to buy in truckloads at better prices, learn from each other, and stay in their family businesses.

This cooperative concept expanded to New England, Pennsylvania and Maryland, but not to the rest of the country, which is the reason that the northeast is still dominated by 700-plus family-owned appliance retailers who can compete with giant national retailers such as Home Depot, Lowes. Eastern Marketing is servicing and providing better profit for these 700 appliance retailers because we don't supply the Xo or Bertazzoni or Blomberg to the big box stores.

We are growing with retailers in the majority of states in the Southeast U.S.

Why Appliance Manufacturers
Succeed or Fail

Recently Craig and I met with the VP of Sales & Marketing of an appliance manufacturer to discuss the possibility of selling their brand. Craig asked the gentleman why he thought other companies making products similar to his were not reaching their goals.

His answer was the typical "salesman's answer"—their price was too high, they lacked financial assistance from their government, and they did not advertise enough.

What he failed to say was quality distribution is difficult to get and that it is still an important factor in success. Manufacturers engineer different types of features and quality levels into their products, but a refrigerator is still a refrigerator, a range is still a range. They are focused on production and management, on controlling costs, quality and supply chains.

But they are a level removed from the dealers who sell and the people who buy those products. That is the vital role that a sound distribution partner can make.

Today, most manufacturers have taken over distribution of their own brands as a way to retain more margin. Nevertheless, they have overlooked a critical factor: corporate structure sales & marketing is just another department vying for resources. At the distributor, it is their exclusive focus. They must excel at it.

2003 Eastern Marketing sold commercial style cooktops, made in France, for $4,999. Diva DeProvence 48"-wide gas ranges and their induction glass cooktops were also made in France and were popular in Europe. After six years, they stopped USA sales because they could not get additional regional distributors willing to introduce new appliance brands.

GREAT FAMILY-OWNED COMPANIES
THAT EVENTUALLY FAILED

Circuit City, Richmond, Virginia: Sam Wurtzel started the busi-ness in 1949, as the Wards Co. His son took over later. It changed from hands-on family management in 1984 to a public company. They expanded to 700 stores with $2 billion in sales. In the year 2000, despite the fact they were the second largest retailer of large appliances in the U S., they announced they were getting out of the appliance business. They continued to close stores, lay people off, and lose more and more money. In 2008, they filed for Chapter 7 bankruptcy with liquidation. One CEO earned $400 million while the company was losing money. They locked their doors in 2009. Their last CEO said that they went out of business only because the banks would not lend them any more money. In my opinion, the family sold their controlling interests in stock, and the banks chose CEOs with top MBAs to run the company. They didn't understand what made Sam Wurtzel successful.

Lechmere Sales, Cambridge, Massachusetts: The company was started by Abraham Cohen and later run by his three sons, before selling out to Dayton Hudson [today's Target stores] in 1965. who held them as a separate subsidiary. They grew to 37 large "super" stores before being bought by Montgomery Ward in 1994. They had as many as 5,000 employees and were, for years, the dominant and best retailer of consumer merchandise in New England, with annual sales of about $800 million. In 1997, the parent corporation, Montgomery Ward, having lost $249 million dollars, closed the group down as part of a bankruptcy reorganization. Lechmere shared the same problem as Circuit City. The family ran the business, until they went public and lost control. The MBA hired to run the company reduced costs by lowering wages of the key employees and totally changed the successful efforts of the families that built the business. Personally, the CEOs did fine financially, but the company failed.

1980 Woods Freezers from Canada.

Tops Appliance, Edison, New Jersey: The company started in 1970 by Les Turchin and expanded to eight Megastores [45,000 to 120,000 sq. ft.] in the metropolitan New Jersey and New York area. By 1990, revenues had grown to $300 million, and two years later, they went public on the NASDAQ, at which time Mr. Turchin relinquished control. Tops hired an MBA from an elite university. He had experience as a VP at Sears. He eliminated all of the most valuable salespeople because he decided to reduce costs to show more initial profit and justify his increase in salary. In 1996, the company lost $15.9 million. It filed Chapter 11 bankruptcy in 2000. In my opinion, as my friend Les Turchin told me, it was the same problem as with Circuit City and Lechmere Sales. He added that when he saw what they were doing to his company, he complained at the board meeting and was told: "Mr. Turchin, you are no longer the majority owner of this company. Please don't tell us what to do. If you don't like what we are doing, don't attend any more board meetings."

Eastern Marketing arranged for Builder Sale with six gas grills on rooftop floor on new building in the Hudson Yards area in Manhattan.

All three of the above are examples of what can happen when new management departs from the core principles that an enterprise is built on. Adding more stores and achieving more sales volume does not guarantee profitability. The stock market interests can rapidly erode profitability.

Internet sales of appliances and TVs have been growing. They represent about 20 percent of the business currently, and that number will continue to grow until it finds a new equilibrium. However. it will never completely replace interacting on a personal level. That is why there is still a shortage of good salespeople at retail and wholesale to explain the features and benefits of consumer appliances and new categories of electronics and appliances. There is always a shortage of good salespeople at the wholesale level, and there is a shortage of good kitchen designers who can sit with consumers and help them turn their ideas into realities. Yes, there is still opportunity in the business, and if I could do it, then . . . YOU CAN TOO.

Done Right, Family Businesses are Wonderful

In 2002, my son Craig took over the leadership of the company and I stepped back into an advisory role. Every company needs just one person to make all the decisions.

In addition to being proud of Craig for all he has accomplished with the business, I am equally proud of the successes of my other son, Robert. Robert is not in the family business because I traditionally believe that having two brothers in the business where only one can be in charge can be a problem. I commend those who can do it, but I could not recommend it. Robert was a successful accountant and CFO and part-owner of a company in the construction business. I love them both for their devotion to their family and their sense of independence and maturity.

In 2007, we were contacted by Bertazzoni from Guastalla, Italy, a manufacturer of cooking products, and a family business since 1882.

They were setting up US distribution and asked us to be their importer and distributor for the Northeast. They have been a wonderful partner. Their strength, like many Italian manufacturers located in northern Italy, has been in design and engineering.

Of all the family businesses I know, I am most impressed with P.C. Richard & Son of Long Island, New York. They are the largest chain of privately-held, family-owned electronics and appliances stores in the United States. They currently have 68 stores located in New York, New Jersey, Connecticut, and Pennsylvania.

KBIS Show at Bertazzoni booth with Alan & Mark Howard from Plessers, Manny Velez & Craig Friedman from EMC and Nicola Bertazzoni.

We have been doing business with P.C. Richard & Son since 1968 when Bill Trawick, who was then the GMM, bought our Sanyo appliances. They competed and won their battles with Newmark & Lewis, Stevens, Friendly Frost, Trader Horn, Tops, Best Buy, Circuit City, and Sears.

They survived because family management guided their business. They hired the best middle management and employees they could find. They invested in a state-of-the-art training facility to help their people excel. They created a top-notch logistics system for fast deliveries. They invested in their own service organization. They maintained good relationships with their suppliers to foster a true sense of partnership, and of course, they always provided the consumer with good values and outstanding service.

They could have easily been torn apart by family differences, but they were not. Greg Richard, of the fourth generation, continues to run the business like his great-grandfather, his grandfather, and his father. They could have sold out to Wall Street and gone public, but they didn't. They deserve everyone's praise and respect for sticking to the basics.

That wise old man with the big cigar and the friendly spirit, A.J. Richard, taught them all that. Whenever I visited their headquarters, I would often see A.J. in the hallway or the reception area. He would always go out of his way to talk to me. He was always genuinely warm and respectful even though I was just "another salesman." More than once he told me that his business could not exist without two things, his suppliers' support, and his customers. He was a special man who understood what it took to make it in this business, and despite his success, he remained humble and approachable.

Every year, I would look forward to the annual P.C. Richard & Son Vendor Appreciation Day and Golf Outing at the family's country club. Presidents and vice-presidents from all the top manufacturers would fly into New York just to be there for the event. If every "work" day was like that one, then no one would ever take time off or consider retiring. At the end of the dinner, the highlight for me was the speech given by A. J. Richard. He would always give an emotional and inspiring speech that would bring everyone in the audience to their feet with applause.

I can never forget the "over the top" black tie affair they had for their 100th Anniversary Celebration in 2009. It was at the Marriott Marquis in New York City. The special guest entertainer for the evening was New Jersey's own Jon Bon Jovi.

The key speaker for the evening was Gregg Richard, the President of P.C. Richard & Son. He looked at the massive audience in their tuxedos and gowns, then with his arms outstretched and fists clenched, declared, "WE DID IT. 100 YEARS IN OUR FAMILY BUSINESSS, AND WE ARE STILL HERE TO CELEBRATE THE OCCASION." He then went on to introduce the many Richard family members present, most of whom were in the company.

It was a thrilling experience for everyone, but it held a special significance for me, as the founder of a family business.

Presented with our company's Founder's Award by my son, Craig.

Before closing this chapter, I would like to add another thank you to A.J. Richard, who always inspired me with his genuine warmth and his quotes. I hope to pass that on to others as well. He always took the time to talk with and listen to all his suppliers, even small ones like us. He always took a keen interest in the products that we were selling to his company. He wanted to know that we were being treated fairly, and what they might do to continually improve the business.

His favorite speech which I always remember,
The Six Most Important Words are: *I admit I made a mistake.*
The Five Most Important Words are: *You did a good job.*
The Four Most Important Words are: *What is your opinion?*
The Three Most Important Words are: *Respect begets respect.*
The Two Most Important Words are: *Thank you.*
The Most Important Word is: *We.*
The Least Important Word is: *I.*
Don't be a bigshot and think you did it all yourself.

EMC Dealers at the Ritz Carlton Resort
in Laguna Niguel, CA to see new Lynx grills.

PICK THE RIGHT PERSON
TO WATCH YOUR BACK

BUSINESS IS ABOUT PEOPLE. THE WRONG ones can cost you dearly as I learned from my ex-partners. However, I was fortunate to always pick the right inside person to help run my sales rep business, both at Marketing East and later, at Eastern Marketing. Without a doubt, it was their hard work and caring efforts backing me up inside the offices that enabled both my companies to be as successful as they were. Knowing that critical aspect of the business was under control freed me to dedicate my time to my customers and suppliers in order to grow more rapidly.

Our first office manager was my wife, Corrine. Fortunately, she came with great experience, having been employed as a receptionist and inside salesperson from the time she graduated high school. She had worked for Golden Electric, a small appliance distributor in Newark. After a couple of years, we moved to NYC and Corrine stepped out of the business, at least temporarily. Years later, she also filled that critical role for a time when I was starting up Eastern Marketing.

My next office manager at Marketing East was Lillian Muldow. Our office was on 7th Ave around the corner from Madison Square

Garden in New York City. Lillian had been the devoted, long-time Administrative Assistant to Artie Heller, the merchandise manager of S. Klein Department Stores, a high-volume department store chain in New York City.

I had seen Lillian in action many times, taking care of three or four emergencies at once and I had a great respect for her professionalism and abilities. She was terrific under pressure, handling problems with deliveries, purchase orders, warranty issues and making sure that merchandise was in the stores for their advertising deadlines. Her experience was precisely what I needed for the business. I worked actively to recruit her for many months. It took me at least a year to convince her to leave, but when S. Klein started reducing staff prior to going out of business, she agreed to join my company.

The next great hire for the position of Office Manager is still our General Manager at Eastern Marketing, Ester Ivanyutin. We knew her because she worked as a bookkeeper for one of our dealers, Regal MagnaMart, in Linden, NJ.

Ester had a wonderful "Can-Do" attitude that set her apart. She was not only good with the books and the computers, but she had no problem stepping in to help our customers, making sales in the store when needed.

She immigrated to the US from Russia. She and her husband lost their good jobs once they applied to leave. They were only permitted to bring a very limited amount of their money with them to their new country. They came with their two very young children and many nights had to sleep in public facilities because they didn't have the money to stay in hotels. But they got here. Ester Ivanyutin overcame all that with intelligence, work ethic, and desire. She left Regal MagnaMart where she was a bookkeeper and part time salesperson to get a degree in computer technology in order to work as a computer consultant and fortunately we were able to convince her to join our team instead.

Companies are a reflection of their people. Pick the right ones, empower them and you will be well on your way to success.

THE PRICE OF SUCCESS

I LEARNED EARLY ON THERE WAS 'No free lunch" in this world. If I hoped to succeed it would entail sacrifices which I was willing to make. Long hours of study, fourteen-hour days on the road prioritizing my work over family which is a difficult trade-off.

There is another side to that "Price of Success" that people in my position may overlook. Other people in your life must also pay that price too and sacrifice as well. It is cause for conflict and hardship and demands a balance that is difficult to accept.

I have been fortunate that I have always enjoyed what I do. I think it has been great fun building my success by helping others achieve their own. It has been incredibly rewarding. I have been to be blessed with my family, particularly my wife, she was and still is my life partner. My family had to have a lot of breakfasts, dinners, and events without me.

Naturally my family has enjoyed the financial benefits of all my labors, but they also endured my long absences. When I took a risk or leap of faith, they jumped right along with me.

There was resentment and jealousy that built up, in particular between a workaholic father and two sons, which took time to reconcile. That's because the absence of time created the problem, so only time could heal it. It wasn't their fault, it was mine. Unfortunately, I will never get back all the time that I missed. I apologize to them, now and forever.

I started out in this message by saying I am the luckiest man alive.

One of the things I am proudest about, with regard to my two sons, is that they have always prioritized their time around their families, in part because of all the time we missed out on together. That hardship made them better men and today we enjoy a far better relationship than I deserve, perhaps. How much luckier could I be?

2006: Dan Schwartz, Karls Appl, John Cioletti, Reno's Appl, Judy Yudin, Yudins Appl, with Craig & Marty at NECO Show.

The Eastern Marketing Appliance
Distributing Business Today

MY SON, CRAIG FRIEDMAN, DOES AN outstanding job as CEO growing the business to be one of the most successful. It is also one of the very few independent distributors still operating.

That is because manufacturers have been sold to larger manufacturers, and when that happens, the new ownership terminates the previous distributors and sales agencies to use their own salespeople to make sales. They may not provide the same level of service to the retailers, they push hard to do business with the Big Box stores, but they then have total control of all their employees.

Our company has sold maybe 35 different brands through the years and we were terminated by most of them because another larger manufacturer bought that company.

Now we sell Bertazzoni kitchen appliances and Blomberg kitchen appliances, and our own Xo grand undercounter beverage centers, wine cellars, range hoods, gas grills, pizza ovens, microwave ovens, garbage disposals, and Wine & Weed beverage long-term storage units, to replace the brands that we had been selling.

We don't sell Big Box stores and do sell 700-plus independent appliance retailers, usually owned and operated by family ownership.

2019: Expo Design luxury home center store [one of 20 stores] with Outdoor Kitchen Display by Eastern Marketing.

We are fortunate to have many of the best people in the business as teammates. A General Merchandise Manager, who is the best in the business. A Director of Sales, overseeing our 11 Field Salespeople who is the hardest working in the business. A Director of Service who is the best in the business. A Service Team with 11 service trucks and 15 service techs who are the best in the business. A knowledgeable Inside Sales Team to answer questions and provide service. An inside Service Support Team that is better than all the others. A very modern, up-to-date website www.easternmarketing.com. And www.xoappliance.com with all the technical and inventory information that the dealer could want, and easily available.

All because what we are selling isn't just merchandise, IT'S MAKING IT EASY TO DO BUSINESS WITH EASTERN MARKETING. AND WE LISTEN.

My not-so-secret suggestions for longevity: You might ask, after 69 years of being in the business, I am still passionate about the selling opportunities in the wholesale appliance business.

2012 Bruno, Blandi, Weissberg, Press, and Friedman.

My *favorite quote is: "If you don't like what you do, but get paid to do it, that's work. But, if you love what you do, you won't have to work a day in your life."*

Afterword

I AM LUCKY TO BE 96 YEARS old with good health and good memories.

My doctors in New Jersey and Florida have both told me that I am in good physical and mental health. They tell me I am an INSPIRATION to all people of advanced age. They ask me every time what I so that they can advise their patients. They both say that I look like I'm in my 70s. That is nice to hear.

Heredity

I believe that genetics is responsible for 50 percent of the answer. The other 50 percent is something that you can affect.

Physical Exercise

Since the age of about 14, I have been a jogger.

For the last 50 years I have been concerned about exercising regularly. Today, my exercise regimen is 15 minutes on the tread mill up to 3.0 mph, three or four days a week to get the heart-beat up to 100 beats per minute; 10 minutes on leg strengthening machines, 10 minutes on upper body strengthening machines,

5 minutes on crunches, 5 minutes on leg stretches, 5 minutes of Yoga type seated relaxation with deep breaths, and only recently I started to do push-ups from the knees. I do 50 push-ups, and finish with 2 minutes on the vibration machine. This is followed by a very hot shower with bending to the count of 12 to touch the ground with the palms of my hands.

I play 9 holes of golf, because I get exhausted after playing 18 holes. I do those two or three times a week. I shoot my age 20 percent of the time. Today I shot 46.

I can only drive the ball 165 yards. I play golf from the forward tees to shoot in the high 90s. As we age, our ability to rebuild and repair our bodies deteriorates. It is much easier to stay in shape, than to get in shape.

Diet

There is an old saying, "You are what you eat." I agree. It is easy to succumb to excesses, but they will eventually catch up to you. Habits like smoking and alcohol can run your health down quickly. The key is moderation. Watch your salt and fat intake, get in the habit of reading labels and take an interest in what goes into the food you consume.

I believe that grapefruits are very healthy. The reason that all our fruits and vegetables are in colors is that whoever created this world meant to encourage us to eat what was colorful, so those foods were all in color.

Fish and chicken are good to eat every week, but meat I eat once a month

A lot of water intake is good. Don't eat after dark and don't eat anything from your 6:00 p.m. dinner time until your morning breakfast.

Sleep

I sleep eight or nine hours a night, and it's difficult to accept that I require a nap every afternoon for two hours. My doctors tell me that it's healthy to be able to sleep like that in the afternoon.

After Corrine died in 2015, I went on a diet and exercise program and lost 30 lbs. I was 5'10" and 192 lbs. but I like my 162 lb. weight today. Consider having the fish or chicken rather than beef and maybe saying, "No thank you" to the dessert menu, or eat fruit for dessert.

Mental Activity

My mind is involved in current and personal events, and with business, including reading books or listening to audiobooks regularly. Reading is a great mental discipline. In addition, I keep up with the activities of our 11 district sales managers and our management team.

Products are always evolving and changing so I continue to learn as much as any of our salespeople about the features and benefits of our new and current appliance brands and the models.

I even have a computer consultant work with me every week for two hours at my home to keep me up to date with technology. It is just as important to exercise the brain as it is to exercise the body. The mind needs to be challenged every day, too. When the eighty-year-olds ask me "What can you possibly learn about computers that you don't already know," I ask them if they know what "Control C and Control V" means? Or, what does Chat GPT or Bing co-pilot mean? When they say that they don't know. I tell them that I didn't know either, but I know now. It's what every 12-year-old knows. That's part of keeping up with computers.

Emotional Health

In 1956, one morning at 9:00 a.m., while playing golf, I found that I had indigestion. My doctor told me the cause was aggravation caused by the business and that if I did not change my ways, I should consider changing my career. If I did not, the problem would only worsen. I loved the work that I was doing, but I didn't love what it was doing to me.

Then, I came to a realization. The work wasn't the problem—how I reacted to it was. I taught myself to relax, telling myself that when you cannot change situations, you can learn to accept them. It was very effective at helping me cope with the day-to-day stresses involved in building the business.

My description to cope is to imagine that you are in your car driving on an interstate highway when the traffic stops. You can't go forward or backwards. You are stuck. Not in control. It is time for you to teach yourself that instead of aggravating yourself in a situation that you can't control, that you relax and either do something productive for business, or you listen to music and wait. It worked for me.

In my personal life, I fell in love with my Corrine in 1954 and that romance lasted for 67 years. Although I have been involved with my sons and their families, her passing created a vacuum in my life. But I have been fortunate to be part of a big business where I can help people improve, help the business grow, and improve with people outside of the business who I respect and who befriended me.

I am interested in continuing to learn, and stay involved with whose company I enjoy.

Not bad for 96 years of life, and who has fulfilled his biggest dreams, and YOU CAN TOO.

My recommendation for young people looking for a lifetime career that is fun, fulfilling and rewarding, is to select the Kitchen Appliance Business because there is a major shortage in talent in:

SALES: long-term wholesale sales, probably starting with a job as a retail salesperson to learn and gain experience

DESIGN: as a kitchen designer or as a house designer working with consumers or architects or builders. Certification is comparatively easy and not expensive.

APPLIANCE SERVICE: as a repair person seeing eight or 10 consumers a day solving their problems with their expensive kitchen appliances. Trade Schools can be a good start. Working as a driver/apprentice can help.

With all the above categories, the opportunities are there because many of today's workers would rather be given the title and be tied to a computer every day, than to be creative and help others . . . and still enjoy above-average income.